The Angolan Economy

Significant Issues Series

SIGNIFICANT ISSUES SERIES papers are written for and published by the Center for Strategic and International Studies.

Series Editors:	David M. Abshire
	Douglas M. Johnston
Director of Studies:	Erik R. Peterson
Director of Publications:	Nancy B. Eddy
Managing Editor:	Roberta L. Howard
Associate Editor:	Yoma Ullman

❖ ❖ ❖

The Center for Strategic and International Studies (CSIS), founded in 1962, is an independent, tax-exempt, public policy research institution based in Washington, D.C. The mission of the Center is to advance the understanding of emerging world issues in the areas of international economics, politics, security, and business. It does so by providing a strategic perspective to decision makers that is integrative in nature, international in scope, anticipatory in its timing, and bipartisan in its approach. The Center's commitment is to serve the common interests and values of the United States and other countries around the world that support representative government and the rule of law.

CSIS, as a public policy research institution, does not take specific policy positions. Accordingly, all views, positions, and conclusions expressed in this publication should be understood to be solely those of the author.

The Center for Strategic and International Studies
1800 K Street, N.W.
Washington, D.C.   20006
Telephone: (202) 887-0200
Fax: (202) 775-3199

The Angolan Economy:
Prospects for Growth in a Postwar Environment

Shawn H. McCormick

THE CENTER FOR STRATEGIC & INTERNATIONAL STUDIES
Washington, D.C.

Significant Issues Series, Volume XVI, Number 5
© 1994 by The Center for Strategic and International Studies
Washington, D.C.   20006
All rights reserved
Printed on recycled paper in the United States of America

Library of Congress Cataloging-in-Publication Data

McCormick, Shawn H.
   The Angolan economy : prospects for growth in a postwar environment / by Shawn H. McCormick.
      p.   cm.   — (Significant issues series, ISSN 0736-7136 ; v.16, no. 5)
ISBN 0-89206-187-1
   1. Angola—Economic conditions—1975–   2. Angola—Economic policy.   3. Angola—Politics and government—1975–   I. title.   II. Series.
HC950.M38   1994
338.9673--dc20   94-11211
                                                                                                  CIP

Contents

Preface	vi
About the Author	vii
Basic Facts about Angola	viii
Map of Angola	x
1. Overview	1
2. Agriculture	10
3. Coffee	17
4. Timber	20
5. Livestock	22
6. Fishing	25
7. Diamonds	29
8. Other Minerals	34
9. Oil	38
10. Hydroelectric Power	45
11. Manufacturing	48
12. Transportation	56
13. Conclusion	64
Sources	66
Appendix: Key Dates in the History of Angola	68

Preface

This addition to the CSIS Significant Issues Series assesses Angola's economic resources and reconstruction prospects sector by sector, as well as the interests and roles of the key foreign governments and entities involved in the country.

This report was initially prepared as an unclassified analytical assessment of the Angolan economy for the U.S. Department of State's Bureau of Intelligence and Research. Originally researched and presented in 1991, the analysis was updated in 1993 and early 1994 for publication by the African Studies Program of the Center for Strategic and International Studies.

About the Author

Shawn H. McCormick is deputy director of the African Studies Program and director of both the Angola Study Group and Nigeria Working Group at the Center for Strategic and International Studies in Washington, D.C. His current research and publications focus on the war in Angola and the country's economic potential and on political issues in Nigeria. McCormick served as an international observer of the September 1992 elections in Angola, the December 1992 elections in Kenya, and the April 1994 elections in South Africa.

The author first visited Angola in August 1990, when he spent eight days in the bush with UNITA forces in Cuando Cubango province and an equal amount of time immediately afterward in the capital, Luanda. A subsequent visit took him to both Luanda and Jamba in August 1991. In August 1992, he was the keynote speaker at a United Nations conference in Luanda on human rights. The following month McCormick served as an election observer in Cuanza Sul province and remained in Angola through early October. His most recent visit was in August 1993. He has also visited Portugal on numerous occasions in relation to events in Angola.

His publications on Angola include "Angola: The Road to Peace" (*CSIS Africa Notes* no. 125, June 1991) and "Angola in Transition: The Cabinda Factor" (*CSIS Africa Notes* no. 137, June 1992). He is preparing a book on the history of relations between Angola and the United States.

Basic Facts about Angola

Population:	10.9 million (1993 estimate)
Capital city:	Luanda (2.9 million)
Average annual population growth:	2.6%
Major languages:	Portuguese (official), Umbundu, Kimbundu, Kikongo, Tchokwe, Ovambo
Religions:	Catholic (51%), Protestant (17%), non-Christian (32%)
Number of universities:	1
Area:	481,354 square miles (1,246,700 square kilometers)
Gross domestic product (GDP):	$8.4 billion (1991 estimate)
Gross national product (GNP) per capita:	$700 (1991 estimate)
Total external debt:	$10.9 billion (1993 estimate)
Monetary unit:	kwanza
Major seaports:	Luanda, Namibe, Lobito, Benguela, Cabinda
Major exports:	petroleum and oil products, diamonds, coffee

Other sources of income, current or potential:	iron ore, phosphates, copper, feldspar, gold, bauxite, uranium
Major imports:	food and beverages, vegetable products, transport equipment, electrical equipment, base metals
Major trading partners, in descending order of importance:	
Imports:	Portugal, Spain, France, United States, United Kingdom, Germany, Belgium/Luxembourg
Exports:	United States, Belgium/Luxembourg, France, United Kingdom, Brazil, Portugal, Germany, Spain

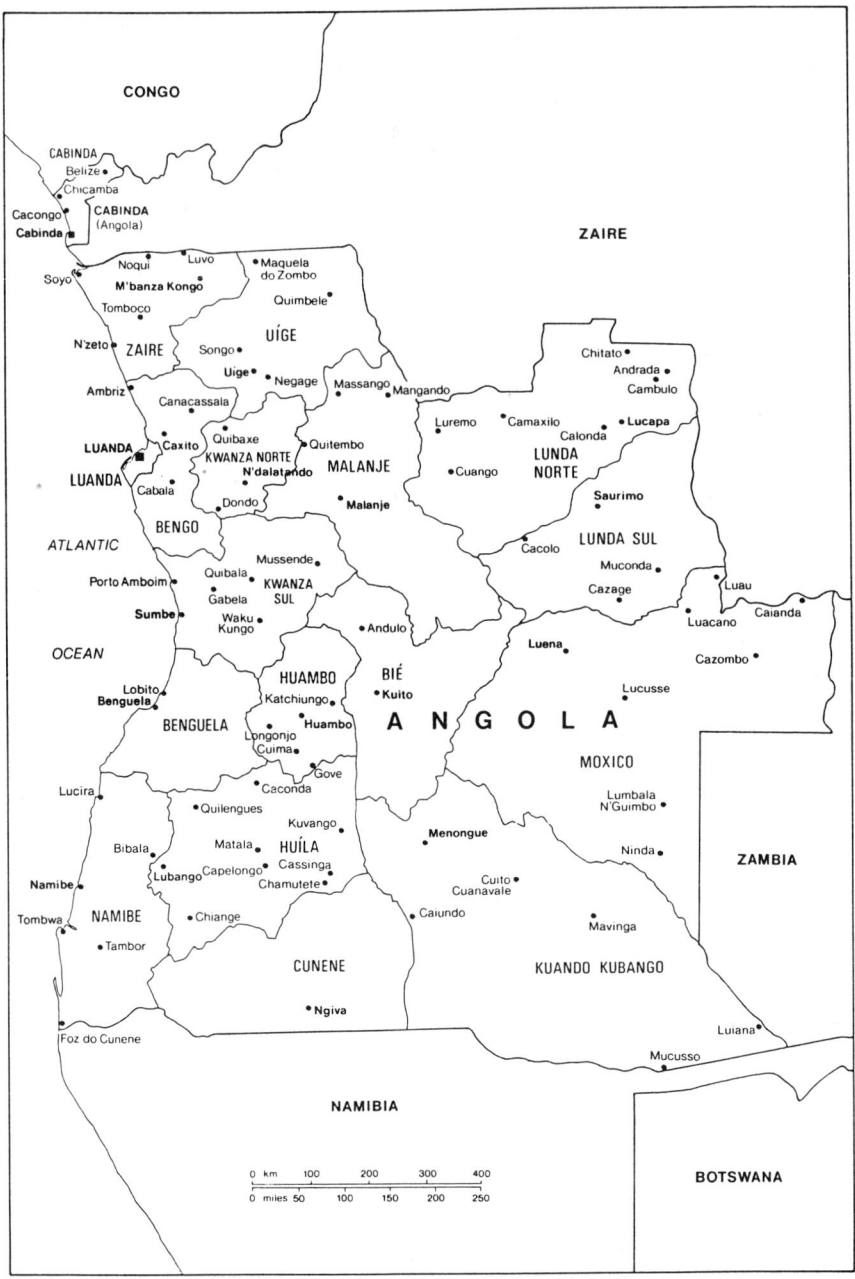

Note: Cuando Cubango, Cuanza Norte, and Cuanza Sul are the Angolan spellings for the provinces shown on this U.S. government map as Kuando Kubango, Kwanza Norte, and Kwanza Sul. The Angolan spellings are used in the text.

1
Overview

Of the five African territories controlled by Portugal during the colonial era, Angola had the greatest economic potential. Its natural resources—including diamonds, coffee, other agricultural products, iron ore, and significant reserves of oil—far surpassed those of Portugal itself. Large-scale exploitation of these resources did not begin until the later years of Portuguese rule, in part because Portugal prevented most non-Portuguese companies from working in Angola prior to the outbreak of the war of independence in 1961.

But this economic potential, which could have made Angola one of the richest countries in Africa, continues to be unrealized because of more than three decades of war. A 14-year anticolonial struggle against Portugal followed by more than 18 years of civil war between the Movimento Popular de Libertação de Angola (MPLA) government and the União Nacional para a Independência Total de Angola (UNITA) guerrilla movement has left Angola with conditions comparable to those in the world's poorest countries. Optimism over Angola's economic prospects following the signing of the May 1991 peace agreement between the MPLA and UNITA have been dashed following the country's return to war as a consequence of UNITA's initial refusal to accept the results of multiparty elections held in September 1992 and initiation of a cycle of violence that led to a resumption of full-scale war.

The end of Portuguese rule in 1975 (see Appendix, "Key Dates in the History of Angola") set in motion a three-way civil war among Angolan nationalist movements that over time resulted in the shattering of the emerging nation's economy. Most of the 350,000 Portuguese settlers fled Angola during the power struggle, draining the country of virtually all of its skilled and semiskilled work force. To make matters worse, many of the departing Portuguese sabotaged sections of the infrastructure, including factories, plantations, and transportation systems, because they could not take them back to Portugal and refused to turn them over to the Africans. What was not destroyed the state in essence inherited from those who abandoned the country.

The events of 1975, the continuation of the colonial pattern of centralized planning by the MPLA government, and the military stalemate that marked much of the post-independence period reduced most economic activity to a fraction of colonial-era levels. From the late 1970s until May 1991, UNITA guerrillas (with considerable South African assistance) carried out economically devastating attacks against infrastructural targets (bridges, roads, railroads, factories, markets, and mineral extraction facilities). This war uprooted a significant portion of the population in critical agricultural areas and shut down the transport sector in important parts of the country.

Moreover, the war forced the MPLA government to divert resources away from economic development. In the later stages of the conflict, an estimated one-half of the Angolan budget was earmarked for defense-related purposes. Only the oil sector, largely located in the coastal Cabinda enclave in the northwest and offshore areas (and protected until 1991 by Cuban forces), enjoyed growth, because of multinational oil companies that negotiated agreements for further development of the country's rich petroleum resources.

The failure of Portugal to facilitate the education and training of all but a handful of Angolans during the colonial era has been among the most damaging legacies of that period. Portuguese-occupied jobs ranged from provincial governors to truck drivers to lottery ticket salesmen. Angolans were left uneducated and simply relegated to low-wage manual-labor employment or often forced labor. The shortage of trained indigenous personnel at independence forced the MPLA government to pay large fees to skilled and semiskilled foreign workers in most sectors, especially mining and diamond production.

Development was also hampered by the MPLA's pursuit of socialist economic policies for more than a decade after it came to power. In the agricultural sector, for example, collectivization served as a disincentive to production, and state control of ports and shipping without qualified personnel caused stagnation in these critical sectors. Price subsidies absorbed governmental expenditures that might otherwise have gone into development. Consumer goods became scarce, corruption flourished, and black markets became the mainstay.

The overvaluation of the kwanza meant that workers were often paid in goods rather than money. Consumer products have often been diverted from the state distribution agencies into "parallel" markets where they are sold at 200 to 300 times the official prices. In the capital city of Luanda alone, two large black-market zones host a flourishing trade in everything from basic food staples to imported suits and refrigerators. It is conservatively estimated that 90 percent of the average household income in Angola is spent in the black market. Although the government devalued the 14-year fixed rate of the kwanza from 29.62 to 6,500 to the dollar, the latest black-market rate stands at more than 110,000.

Since coming to power in 1975, the MPLA has exhibited a pragmatic willingness to establish constructive relations with foreign companies, especially those involved in the country's critical oil sector. Over the past half-decade, that pragmatic streak has always contrasted strongly with the regime's formal commitment to Marxist rhetoric on a range of issues.

By the mid-1980s, a combination of depressed oil prices, continuing war, and a virtual breakdown in all other sectors of the economy was forcing the government to reconsider its dependence on central planning. The initial foundations for a revamping of the government's economic policies were laid down at the MPLA's Second Party Congress in 1985. Although the MPLA formally reaffirmed its commitment to socialism at that time, it acknowledged that the civil war was not the sole cause of the country's economic woes.

In 1987, the government announced sweeping plans for an Economic and Financial Restructuring Program (Saneamento Económico e Financeiro, or SEF). The two broad components of the SEF were stabilization measures and restructuring. The proposed stabilization measures included

- reducing the state budget deficit
- new methods of financing the state deficit
- restructuring the public sector
- strengthening the financial system
- reforming domestic credit policies
- rescheduling the external debt
- liberalization and adjustments of controlled prices
- exchange-rate adjustment
- stricter control in monetary and fiscal policies

The planned structural reforms included

- an increased role and more autonomy for the private sector
- revised rules for foreign investment
- improvements in the existing socialist system of planning

Achieving the goals of the SEF was expected to depend upon implementation of such essential macroeconomic measures as (1) allowing prices to be determined by the market rather than price controls, (2) depreciation of the exchange rate, and (3) greater control over the money supply. A few of the proposed changes were implemented. Others awaited the enactment of key legislation. Lack of government commitment and the dismissal of those who developed the SEF program ultimately doomed this initiative.

In September 1990 the government renewed the abandoned SEF program under the title of the Government Action Program. Six measures were undertaken:

- cutting of unnecessary government expenditures,
- imposition of an across-the-board 10 percent customs duty and a 400 percent increase in international airfares on the state-owned air-carrier,
- lifting of price controls on all but 25 items,
- a 100 percent devaluation of the kwanza (not implemented until March 1991),
- an increase in imports to promote consumption, and
- implementation of a currency exchange replacing the kwanza with the "new kwanza" in order to reduce the money supply. Only 5 percent of the old currency held by an individual or company could be exchanged for new kwanzas; the rest was "converted" into government bonds paying 8 percent interest. This move caused frustration and confusion among the populace. The government subsequently increased the supply of new kwanzas, further driving down the value of the Angolan currency.

In addition, President José Eduardo dos Santos said that Angola, at the time the sole African country remaining aloof from the International Monetary Fund (IMF) and the World Bank, would now apply for membership in both international organizations. It was accepted into the two institutions and was quickly able to secure rescheduling of $1.8 billion in debt. A further $750 million was rescheduled through 1992, but in the absence of a comprehensive structural adjustment program with the IMF no such further efforts were permitted.

In November 1990, some 700 members of the Angolan business community gathered in Luanda, where they heard President dos Santos promise assistance to the indigenous private sector. An immediate measure taken in response to the concerns expressed at the meeting was the release of 50 percent of the corporate bank deposits frozen during the currency exchange; the authority of banks to give credit (suspended during the exchange) was restored.

Another result of the meeting was the creation of several new financial institutions as part of the government's effort to reform the banking sector. The Banco de Comércio e Indústria (BCI) was established to cater to the credit needs of the manufacturing sector, and it was agreed that another credit institution would be created to service the agricultural, livestock, and fisheries sectors. In an effort to spur domestic investment, the government extended the right to engage in foreign-exchange operations to the Banco Popular de Angola (BPA), a state-owned commercial bank, whereas before only the country's central bank, the Banco Nacional de Angola (BNA), had been allowed to do so. This liberalization measure was meant to address the private sector's need for foreign exchange to buy production inputs.

Prospects that Angola was beginning to emerge from war and socialism after the signing of the Bicesse Peace Accords in May 1991 prompted numerous foreign investors to investigate opportunities in the country. Without a comprehensive overhaul of the economy and a revised investment code, however, most foreign corporations (with the notable exception of oil companies) remained wary of making substantial investments. The renewed fighting is at present an even more significant barrier to foreign investment.

In September 1991, UNITA released two important documents on economic policy that would become particularly relevant should UNITA reach a position from which it could influence the economic policies of the country. These documents, one concerning investment and the other general economic policy, seemed to reiterate UNITA's long-proclaimed dedication to a free-market economy with limited government control in the long term, in which foreign investment would be encouraged and privatization viewed as the cure for the inefficient and bloated bureaucracy that evolved under MPLA rule.

The most noteworthy of the differences between the proposed economic policies of UNITA and the reformed MPLA was UNITA's attitude toward contracts with foreign companies. UNITA openly expressed its disapproval of foreign contracts concluded during the transition period before the 1992 elections and warned that any and all contracts deemed contrary to the Angolan national interest would be reassessed should UNITA ever come to power. In essence, UNITA officials reserved the right to review all contracts to investigate whether or not corruption might have been involved. As one senior UNITA official commented, "If a company didn't bribe anyone, then they have nothing to worry about."

UNITA characterized its proposed economic policies as "systemic and structural," implying that MPLA attempts at reform since 1985 had been insufficiently comprehensive and thus ineffective. In a meeting at the Overseas Private Investment Corporation during UNITA president Jonas Savimbi's October 1991 visit to Washington, his secretary for finance and economics, Dr. Fatima Roque, noted that a 1991 World Bank report on Angola included the following observation: "To date, no significant economic reforms have been implemented."

Dr. Roque, who was essentially responsible for the formulation of UNITA economic policy, offered four reasons for the MPLA's failure to achieve much economic progress:

- lack of political courage
- inability to formulate a comprehensive macroeconomic reform program
- resistance on the part of those benefiting from the status quo
- the lack of an economic team with both the technical skills and the political authority to implement an effective program

As many officials in the Angolan Ministry of Finance have commented to this author, it is relatively easy for UNITA to criticize the MPLA's reform attempts because UNITA has never been in a position to implement economic reforms in such a large and complex bureaucracy. Moreover, a number of foreign observers criticized Roque's own plan as being "too academic" and not totally grounded in reality. Given the social and economic disruption (e.g., at least 100,000 deaths, an estimated 2 million displaced persons, widespread hunger) that has accompanied the renewed civil conflict, the debate is moot for now.

Since the resumption of warfare in late October 1992, the government has blocked all efforts by reformist elements to address the country's macroeconomic distortions. There is no transparency or accountability in the nation's fiscal operations. The significant increase in the money supply and a ballooning budget deficit have pushed the inflation rate beyond 1,800 percent annually and uncontrollable hyperinflation is a real possibility. Corruption, previously termed "manageable" by one senior IMF official, is now at alarming levels. A small group of well-connected MPLA officials has virtually unlimited access to state resources, while the urban masses subsist largely on foreign donations of food or black-market activities. The rural populace relies on subsistence agriculture or occasional deliveries of international assistance to survive.

Because of excessive government spending in the lead-up to the September 1992 elections and an unwillingness to adopt an economic reform program acceptable to the IMF, the dos Santos regime found itself forced to seek short-term financing to fund its war effort (official 1992 debt reached $9.6 billion and mushroomed to an estimated $10.9 billion in 1993). Unfortunately for the future of Angola, the government mortgaged at least three years of future oil revenues on unfavorable terms in order to procure goods, mainly military supplies. Ninety percent of current government expenditures are defense related. A lack of coordination and accountability on the procurement front has led to the duplicate purchasing of individual items and massive corruption on the part of senior military officers and politicians. The government has never undertaken to prosecute those government or military officials involved in the corruption. Taken together, these policies have seriously frustrated various international financial institutions and bilateral donors.

Compounding this problem is the grave humanitarian situation in the country. According to United Nations (UN) estimates, at least 1,000 people were dying each day either directly or indirectly due to war in mid and late 1993. An additional 3 million, more than one-quarter of the population, will be at risk of starvation in 1994 if massive food deliveries are not forthcoming (the 1992 and 1993 planting seasons were missed due to the resumption of war). Starvation is occurring now in fertile areas and people are even dying of malnutrition in Luanda. The mortality rate at Luanda's central Josina Machel Hospital due to malnutrition was 70 percent in June 1993. The mortality rate for children under the age of five stands at 292 per 1,000, the highest such number in the world. Both the government and UNITA have shown a gross indifference to the plight of the people of Angola.

In early 1994, the government announced the launching of a new program to revitalize the economy of the country. Its cornerstones included instituting a market economy, liberalizing economic activity, and reducing the weight of the state business sector. The program also included adoption of a fluctuating exchange rate system for the national currency. Goals set for the first year included increasing the gross national product (GNP) by 2.5 percent, decreasing public consumption by 35 percent, and maintaining inflation at 250 percent. To achieve these impressive figures, the government said it was "counting on the private activity of Angolan and foreign entrepreneurs."

The Economic and Social Program of 1994 will only be as successful as the political forces in the Angolan government allow. Lack of political support doomed the SEF program in the previous decade and squelched reform efforts in 1991, resulting in the resignation of perhaps Angola's most talented and qualified minister of finance, Aquinaldo Jaime. Even if initial steps are taken to implement the 1994 program, the government's commitment to the announced goals will be tested when negative repercussions eventually reach the populace. One positive element is that the 1994 effort is being spearheaded by Eduardo Severim de Morais, a well-qualified technocrat and economist who is deputy minister of planning and economic coordination.

The prospects for growth in the Angolan economy revolve around seven key points:

1. Above all else, the military conflict must end.
2. Such a cessation of hostilities should then lead to the creation of a stable political system acceptable to the combatants and other political forces in Angolan society.
3. The government created through this peace process must adopt a credible economic structural reform program.
4. The international community would then have a responsibility to lend assistance to this fledgling polity.

5. At this juncture, foreign investors would have the opportunity to develop projects in the country in areas beyond the petroleum sector.

6. The government must give priority attention to the rehabilitation of the nation's infrastructure, without which economic activity will be largely limited to the coastal cities.

7. Development of the country's human resources is another critical need.

Economic recovery in Angola will not occur suddenly. Careful planning, commitment to reform, and diversified foreign investment in all sectors will gradually help Angola to realize its potential as one of Africa's most prosperous nations and an engine for regional economic growth.

2
Agriculture

Angola's climatic diversity provides niches for both tropical and semitropical crops—bananas, beans, corn, cotton, manioc, millet, palm oil, potatoes, sorghum, sunflower, tobacco, and sisal (Angola was the world's third largest sisal producer prior to independence). Estimates of arable land range from 5 to 8 million hectares. At present, however, only 3 percent of this potentially productive area is being cultivated in a country where it is probable that 75 percent of Angolans depend on farming for their livelihood.

The colonial government encouraged Portuguese settlers rather than the indigenous population to develop the agricultural sector. Because Lisbon was unable to attract large numbers of would-be Portuguese farmers to Angola, slave and forced labor became the mainstay of the large plantations. Even after the abolition of these inhumane practices (slavery in the nineteenth century and forced labor in 1961), most Angolans continued to work on plantations or to practice subsistence agriculture. The ratio of land used by Portuguese farmers to that used by indigenous farmers was 100 to 1. Angola gradually became self-sufficient in the production of all crops except wheat and began exporting surplus corn.

The mass exodus of the Portuguese following independence in 1975 caused havoc in the agricultural sector. Most of the plantations were abandoned and such key support industries as marketing and transportation collapsed for lack of trained personnel. The (highly exploitative) national distribution system of "bush traders" that operated during the colonial era and served as the link between farmers and processors was never matched by the national distribution agencies set up by the new government after 1975 to supply tools and consumer goods.

Price controls served as another disincentive to production, shifting the flow of goods and trade from the formal to the informal sector and encouraging the formation of a substantial parallel market. Government statistics show that although some 70 to 80 percent of the population is engaged in small-scale or subsistence agricultural production, this group generates a mere 20 percent of the Angolan GNP. The World Bank estimates, however, that this 20 percent accounts for only that part of agricultural production that is reported to the government, which may represent as little as 10 to 15 percent of actual production.

The civil war that followed independence further compounded problems in agricultural production. Access to rural areas was impeded, the infrastructure devastated, and most major roads became virtually impassable. In addition, over 2 million Angolans sought refuge in neighboring countries, urban areas, or as *dislocados* (displaced persons). The MPLA regime was forced to divert badly needed resources from the agricultural sector to the military.

The government came to recognize the country's deficiencies in this area and took steps to address them. In 1984 it approved an emergency plan to reduce the state role in food production by transforming state farms into peasant associations. Agricultural development stations were created in rural areas to give human, technical, and financial support (including fertilizer, seeds, training, and other production inputs) to these associations.

Unfortunately, these stations have proved to be no more efficient than other state agricultural institutions. Not-yet-implemented SEF guidelines include such agriculture-relevant changes as price liberalization, greater private-sector participation (particularly in transportation, retailing, and wholesaling), new credit facilities, more-decentralized planning, and substantive devaluation of the Angolan currency. The restoration of peasants' confidence, which has been severely shaken by government policies and war, will be a crucial precondition for the production of surpluses for the market.

Production of cassava, corn, millet, and sorghum stood at an estimated 25 to 35 percent of pre-independence levels prior to the resumption of war in October 1992, which coincided with the start of the planting season. Production of cotton, groundnuts, palm oil, sisal, and tobacco remains at less than 10 percent of pre-1975 levels (see table 2.1). Angola is no longer an exporter of agricultural goods and must rely on imports and food aid to avert famine.

The agricultural sector has impressive potential, as the following examples illustrate:

Table 2.1
Comparison of Agricultural Production Levels before and after Independence
(in tons)

Product	Maximum Output	
	Pre-independence	Post-independence
Bananas	399,000 (1973)	114,000 (1991)
Beans	65,500 (1971)	2,452 (1986)
Maize	710,000 (1971)	299,000 (1991)
Cotton	86,015 (1971)	3,000 (1991)
Manioc	1,134,262 (1971)	250,000 (1987)
Sorghum/Millet	74,000 (1971)	59,000 (1991)
Palm Oil	20,000 (1973)	560 (1986)
Potatoes	138,757 (1971)	8,000 (1987)
Sisal	47,920 (1971)	1,000 (1991)
Sunflower	21,008 (1972)	120 (1986)
Tobacco	4,800 (1973)	114 (1986)
Wheat	22,500 (1971)	3,000 (1991)

Source: UNDP/WB Report No. 7283–ANG, p. 346 and *Angola to 2000*, pages 106 and 110.

- **Bananas**, which can be grown in many parts of the country and were first commercially grown in the 1960s near Benguela, would do especially well in coastal regions. In areas subject to drought, however, irrigation systems would be needed.

- **Beans**, another element in the local diet, come in many forms and can be grown throughout the country. The regions that are most suitable for this crop are the central plateaus and the northern provinces.

- **Cotton** grows in many areas of the country, including the Cassange Basin and eastward to Malanje. Agronomists advise that it could also be developed farther south along the Cunene river basin, where the climate is semiarid.

- **Maize**, mainly grown and consumed in the central region, could also be planted in the southwest, which is capable of producing 90,000 tons per year within four years, enough to supply the entire population of that area.

- **Manioc** is a key staple in the northern provinces of the country and is currently grown in large farms near Luanda. The fertile soils eastward across the Luanda plateau are also viewed as suitable for manioc.

- **Millet** does well in the sandy regions of Cunene and Cuando Cubango provinces and could be grown along the entire southern border.

- **Palm oil** comes from trees in the humid valleys of the northwest. Once an important part of the northwestern diet, palm oil could have a strong future.

- **Potatoes** are mainly planted in the central regions of Angola, but could also be produced in the coastal regions of Benguela and Namibe where climatic conditions are more favorable.

- **Sisal** is harvested in areas near the Cuanza river and further south toward Lobito. Both locations have the additional advantage of access to reasonably reliable transportation. Production is currently negligible, but could be significantly increased.

- **Sunflower** has been grown and processed in Malanje, Cuanza Sul, and Benguela provinces, but additional potential exists on soils lying farther south into the province of Namibe.

- **Tobacco** is raised on small plots and large farms near rivers throughout the southwest and in Malanje. In more peaceful times, processing plants in Luanda and Benguela handled the entire output. Tobacco could also be grown farther east from the coast.

- **Wheat** is cultivated mainly in the central highlands. Cooler temperatures in Huíla province once caused problems for farmers who wanted to expand production there, but current research has found possible solutions to many of these difficulties.

The development of the agricultural sector would require not only an infusion of capital and technology, but patience as well. Initially, existing farms could be utilized to bring the country's agricultural output up to pre-independence levels. Even this, however, would be difficult without the rehabilitation of the internal transportation system. Moreover, detailed assessments of given crops and proposed areas of cultivation would be required before large-scale planting of new land.

Prior to the resumption of war in October 1992, a number of projects were initiated to assist in rehabilitating the agricultural sector. Unfortunately, all have been suspended. In August 1991, the Ministry of Agriculture, with Spanish funding support, allotted agricultural plots to 24 war refugee families originally from Huambo and Bié provinces. The project began with an initial investment of $1 million and was supported by a budget of $800,000 from Spain and 50 million kwanza from the Angolan government. Project engineers calculated that the land allotted was worth more than 2 million kwanzas per hectare. Although the farmers involved in this particular program were not allowed to sell or lease their plots, the government's stated long-term plan was to restore private land ownership as a spur to agricultural productivity.

The United Nations Food and Agriculture Organization (UNFAO) and the United Nations Development Program (UNDP) initiated a project to rehabilitate vegetable and fruit production in Luanda, Bengo, and Cuanza Sul provinces. The Italian government offered $894,000 in funds for this rehabilitation project. A similar pilot program was planned for Huíla province, where farmers were to receive essential production tools, such as hoes, buckets, machetes, and animal-driven equipment. In addition, the UNDP and the UNFAO planned to create some form of credit institution to facilitate the distribution of these assets.

This UNFAO and UNDP initiative, one of the most far-reaching ever implemented in southern Angola, also called for establishing a network of retail stores to sell the produce and revitalize the commercial division of the agricultural sector. The UN initiative would also have addressed the training of seasonal workers, managers, Farmers' Association accountants, and administrators of rural extension programs, agricultural systems, and development strategies.

Production of food for domestic consumption must be a priority. Due to war and drought, the 1990 cereal harvest (251,000 tons) satisfied only 39 percent of the country's total needs (637,000 tons). The April 1991 to March 1992 cereal harvest was 367,000 tons, but estimated total domestic cereal needs were at least 650,000 tons. The 1993 harvest statistics were only 321,000 tons, and 1994 projections hover near 300,000 tons. In such a case, food aid requirements will reach 335,000 tons in 1994 and slightly more in 1995. The government request to the international community for food aid has risen fivefold since 1983.

A major problem that will plague any effort to rehabilitate the agricultural sector is the widespread and indiscriminate sowing of land mines that took place throughout the countryside during more than three decades of anticolonial and civil war. Most mines were buried on footpaths leading either to rivers where people (mostly women and children) obtain water or to small agricultural plots used for subsistence farming. Land mines were planted by 10 separate armies, including the Portuguese, the MPLA, UNITA, the Frente Nacional de Libertação de Angola (FNLA), Cuba, Zaire, South Africa, the South West Africa People's Organization (SWAPO), the African National Congress (ANC), and various armed factions of the Frente de Libertação do Enclave de Cabinda (FLEC). It is estimated that there are 10 million of these mines in all—roughly one per Angolan citizen—and maps for less than 20 percent of them.

The country has at least 60,000 amputees—the highest number and percentage in the world. As one example of how bad the situation is, the government currently lacks the technology to locate and deactivate an estimated 100,000 plastic mines sown around the city of Mavinga (in Cuando Cubango province) alone.

The formation of the Joint Political and Military Commission under the terms of the May 1991 peace agreement led to the creation of a subcommission tasked with organizing a national campaign to remove mines. A joint MPLA-UNITA team reportedly deactivated 7,000 antitank and antipersonnel mines prior to the September 1992 elections, allowing for the temporary resumption of traffic on most of Angola's main roads.

Rehabilitation of the agricultural sector is critical for employment and food security. It is also an important element in helping to rejuvenate industries related to agricultural production. It is indeed ironic that Zimbabwe, currently regarded as the "breadbasket" of southern Africa, has less than one-quarter (76,000 sq. km.) of the arable land available in Angola (325,000 sq. km.), but produces several times more agricultural products than does Angola. A coordinated effort to rehabilitate the agricultural sector following the implementation of a peace agreement will turn Angola into the largest producer of agricultural products in the region.

3
Coffee

During the colonial era Angola's main cash crop was coffee. In fact, Angola was the world's third largest producer of coffee and the second largest producer in Africa. Until 1973, when it was overtaken by oil, coffee was the main export earner. Although there were many family farms, coffee was grown mainly on large plantations with thousands of workers in Cuanza Norte, Cuanza Sul, Luanda, and Uíge provinces. At the peak of production in 1973, the coffee sector exported almost 220,000 tons and employed more than 250,000 workers.

With the transfer of power in 1975, most of the 2,500 coffee plantations were abandoned by their Portuguese owners and subsequently nationalized by the government. Because most of the beans that year went unpicked, pest infestation and root fungi caused extensive damage to the bushes. The post-independence MPLA regime decided to nationalize the plantations, but Ovimbundus (who historically made up the majority of migrant pickers) refused to return from the central highlands to the coffee-growing regions in the north because they feared reprisals and retribution from the Kimbundu and Kikongo residents of these regions (because Ovimbundu-dominated UNITA had fought against the new Kimbundu-dominated MPLA government in Luanda). The Ovimbundu migrant workers also feared reprisals from UNITA rebels who began planting antipersonnel mines in government-controlled areas to discourage agricultural production.

Drought, bureaucracy, neglect of the coffee-producing areas, and inadequate transportation facilities compounded these problems and led to a drastic reduction in the amount of coffee produced in the early post-independence period. In 1981, less than 24,000 tons were brought to market and the figure decreased to under 11,000 tons in 1984. Production then fell to 5,000 tons in 1991 and only 3,000 tons in 1993, less than 2 percent of the record production in 1973.

State-owned plantations (which were organized into 33 state enterprises in the early 1980s) produce about 60 percent of the annual output, with another 35 percent coming from peasant farms and 5 percent from larger private estates. Although the dense semideciduous forests covering much of the country are well suited to coffee production, growing is mostly limited to the relatively small Dembos-Uite and Libolo-Amboim areas. Soils suitable for robusta coffee production also exist in savanna areas near these forests.

Most of the country's coffee bushes are more than 40 years old and past their prime. For Angola to regain its position as a leading coffee exporter, these bushes would have to be replaced at considerable expense, and it would be three years before the new bushes yielded any beans. Even so, coffee remains (as it was prior to independence) Angola's third largest export, exceeded only by oil and diamonds. Whereas the United States was the largest importer of Angolan coffee in the colonial era, the main buyers of the decreased output in recent years have been Portugal and Spain.

During the 1980s, several foreign investors became involved in Angolan coffee production. In 1985, France's Caisse Centrale de Coopération Économique lent the government over $5 million to improve the technical facilities for coffee production and support studies on coffee growth. In 1988, an agreement was signed to supply the Soviet Union with 6,000 tons of coffee annually (if possible) in exchange for consumer goods, equipment, and investment in various unspecified forms.

World coffee prices fell dramatically in July 1989 when the International Coffee Organization's export quota system collapsed. That year, Angola's coffee export earnings once again dropped. The coffee industry, having entered the 1980s with the annual crop yielding $164 million, found itself 10 years later earning a mere $4 million.

Among other factors, government price controls prevented farmers from making a satisfactory profit and thus removed most incentives for growing coffee. Because growing cassava for the informal market is more profitable than producing coffee to be sold in the formal market at the official rate, longtime coffee farmers have begun uprooting their bushes to grow cassava.

In search of some relief, the government announced a privatization program in 1990. The government began negotiating with Portuguese, U.S., and British companies to sell the larger state-owned coffee plantations in Cuanza Norte and Benguela provinces; smaller plantations have already been sold to Angolan farmers and negotiations on medium-sized plantations began in early 1992. Although 100 percent foreign ownership of the individual coffee plantations is not prohibited, the government maintains its desire to keep overall foreign ownership to a maximum of 30 to 40 percent. In August 1991, the government offered to sell 33 large coffee plantations; the foreign investment proposals received so far have averaged $2.5 million each.

The depressed world market price for coffee is a significant barrier to increased production. Foreign investors may also find the costs of replacing existing insect-infested bushes prohibitive. In short, the coffee sector is not expected to make much of a contribution to the overall economy in the near term beyond the employment of seasonal manual labor.

4
Timber

Valuable tree species can be found in many regions of Angola. The Maiombe rain forest in Cabinda is rich in precious woods such as rosewood, ebony, and African sandalwood. The Dembos forest in the northwestern section of Angola abounds with mahogany, tola, and mulberry trees. Both of these dense, humid forests have been virtually untapped since independence (except perhaps by the Cubans while the latter were in Cabinda).

Other regions of the country also have significant timber reserves. The northern sections of Uíge and Zaire provinces produce panga-panga. Sections of Moxico and Cuando Cubango provinces in the Kalahari are the source of expensive woods such as girassonde and mussibi. In addition to these natural forests, almost 150,000 hectares of eucalyptus, cypress, and pine plantations exist at elevations above 1,200 meters in the central section of the country.

Production, which stood at 229,128 cubic meters in 1960, rose to over 418,000 in 1970 and to almost 554,000 in 1973; more than half of this came from Cabinda. By 1974, timber exports were generating $11 million per year, and wood pulp an additional $33 million.

Following independence in 1975, the export of timber and timber products ceased until the new government could revamp the methods of production and transport that had been established by the Portuguese. A search was also undertaken for new logging methods that would permit a more rational exploitation of Angolan timber resources. By 1981, production had reached almost 40,000 cubic meters. With technical assistance from Cuba, a forestry company was established in Cabinda in 1983. Production levels jumped to over 115,000 cubic meters in 1984 (more than double the 1983 figure of 57,000 cubic meters) but dropped slightly to 113,000 cubic meters in 1985. Due to the war, this figure fell precipitously to 28,000 cubic meters by 1988 and had declined an additional 2,500 cubic meters by 1991. Production of all types of timber was severely hampered throughout much of the 1980s by UNITA and FLEC attacks on the producing areas themselves and on transportation facilities.

Interestingly, UNITA also benefited from the export of timber, but on the opposite side of the country in Cuanda Cubango province. For several years, in addition to diamonds, timber provided resources with which UNITA could import such items as food, tools, clothing, and weapons. The independence of Namibia in March 1990 dealt a quick blow to this process, however, because the land route by which the hardwoods were exported was shut down. According to UNITA, the Aurora sawmill, some two hours' drive from Jamba, produced 150,000 cubic meters in 1988, but its annual output dropped to 5,000 cubic meters in 1990.

In 1988 the World Bank designated Cabinda as the province whose timber sector would benefit most in the short term from development. Proximity of the forests to the ports, the quality of the region's existing infrastructure, and the high quality of timber are major reasons for the focus on Cabinda's potential.

Although some rehabilitation of milling facilities is necessary, this need not be a prohibitively expensive proposition. For example, in 1990 an automatic sawmill in Cabinda capable of processing 40 cubic meters of timber in an eight-hour workday was assembled in only 45 days by Italian and Angolan technicians at a cost of roughly $1 million.

With proper development schemes, it is estimated that Angola could sustain mills and wood-pulp plants in a variety of locations throughout the country. Expansion of timber plantations in the central highlands region to produce additional eucalyptus, cypress, and pine is also feasible. In sum, this sector of the Angolan economy is well positioned to generate steady employment and capital flows for the foreseeable future.

5
Livestock

Cattle were raised by African pastoralists in southwestern Angola long before the arrival of the Portuguese. Over the course of the following centuries, a system of exchanging goods from Europe for cattle was developed between the colonizers and the herdsmen. Impressed by the potential profits, some of these Portuguese merchants became ranchers themselves. Whereas the indigenous people were nomadic, the Portuguese raised their cattle on permanent farms and focused on commercialization.

For most of the colonial era, cattle production was inhibited by an inconsistent supply of water. Output fluctuated according to seasonal rainfall because cattle were less healthy and less well fed during dry seasons. The Portuguese solved this problem in the 1950s by tapping underground water supplies and building water storage tanks in preparation for the dry seasons. This permitted cattle to be raised not only near rivers, but also in more rural areas to which the water could be pumped. By the time of Angola's transition to statehood in 1975, grazing areas had increased from 5,000 to 20,000 hectares and the number of beef cattle had expanded from 1.8 million to 2.8 million. Another major factor that contributed to increased production in this period was Portuguese success in limiting the spread of the trypanosomiasis disease carried by the tsetse fly.

The livestock sector did not escape the negative economic effects of decolonization. Virtually all of the Portuguese meatpackers and ranchers (who had for the most part supplanted indigenous pastoralists) fled the country, often slaughtering their animals and destroying their facilities. The simultaneous departure of most merchants to Portugal effectively ended the system by which livestock were exchanged by pastoralists for goods. A large number of cattle were also taken across the border to Namibia by South Africans.

The departure of the Portuguese also meant the end of the cattle vaccination programs they had pioneered to limit disease. Beef production sank from 24,500 tons per year before independence to 3,500 tons in 1987. This figure recovered slightly to 7,180 tons in 1991. Whereas Angola had been an exporter of meat before independence, more than 18,000 tons were imported in 1986 and an annual average of 20,000 tons in 1987–1990—even though there were estimated to be 3.4 million cattle in the country.

The drought of the late 1980s and 1990 put the livestock sector under further stress. It affected the central and southern cattle-raising areas of Cuanza Sul, Bié, Huambo, Cuando Cubango, and Cunene (the most important ranching area, where over 300,000 head of cattle died).

In an effort to boost production in the livestock sector, the Angolan government asked the 10-nation Southern African Development Coordination Conference (which in August 1992 became the Southern African Development Community [SADC]) for $80 million in 1991 to help fund a livestock development project. The money was slated for the rehabilitation of cattle water sources and abattoirs, the establishment of a network of cold storage facilities, and the promotion of cattle marketing in the southern provinces of Benguela, Cunene, Huíla, and Namibe, where there were suitable grazing lands free of tsetse flies. The resumption of war, however, has postponed implementation of this program.

The potential for increased cattle production is substantial. Cunene, Huíla, and Namibe provinces have a tradition of successful pastoralism. According to the results of a recent study, traditional African pastoralists were much more productive than Portuguese ranchers, which leads to the conclusion that the revitalization of the sector would require little government investment or attention. A regular supply of water, however, will prove to be elusive in the short term because wells, dams, and water pools were systematically destroyed by UNITA during the civil war. Fortunately, the locations of these facilities are known. Thus, money will not have to be spent on a search for water sources; rather, it can be put directly into a rebuilding effort.

It may also be possible to extend cattle production to new areas. In the latter years of colonial rule, Huambo province attracted increased Portuguese interest because of its supply of water and grazing areas. Several hundred cattle per day were slaughtered at a facility operating in the city of Huambo in this period. Further west, along the coast and above Balombo Falls, thousands of hectares of prairie land may prove valuable for raising livestock. During the colonial period, this area was a lucrative ranching zone where cattle and karakul sheep were raised for commercial purposes.

Another division of the livestock sector that warrants renewed attention is dairy cows. Before independence, Portuguese entrepreneurs constructed three modern, well-equipped creameries to produce pasteurized and sterilized milk, butter, and cheese. The largest of these facilities, located at Cela-Catofe in Cuanza Sul province, had 60,000 cows that produced 120,000 liters of milk per day. The other two produced 30,000 and 15,000 liters of milk per day. Smaller and less advanced centers were constructed near Benguela, Lobito, and Luanda. If these facilities were to become fully functional again, dairy production could make a significant contribution to the country's development and public health.

Goats and pigs are found in towns and villages across Angola, but the highest concentration is near Luanda because of the large consumer market in the nation's capital. The number of goats and pigs before independence stood at 872,000 and 500,000 respectively. In 1988, the figures were 975,000 and 480,000 respectively. Here too a potential for significant growth exists.

In total, the livestock sector is an important link in the Angolan national economy and its rehabilitation should occur with limited external assistance.

6
Fishing

Angola is in a position to reap major benefits from its more than 1,600 kilometers of coastline along the Atlantic Ocean. Most of the developed harbors are in the southern part of the country, where the cold Benguela Current meets the warm Agulhas Current. Plankton is abundant in this region and attracts horse mackerel, tuna, and sardines, which account for 90 percent of all fish harvested. The Portuguese developed ports in Namibe, Tombwa, Lucira, and Lobito to exploit the rich waters.

The largest recorded catch during the colonial era was in 1972, when just over 599,000 metric tons of fish were hauled from the ocean, most of it to be frozen, canned, or salted for export. Production for export in 1974 amounted to more than 60,000 metric tons of fish meal worth $19.5 million, over 10,000 metric tons of fish oil worth $3.2 million, and almost 35,000 metric tons of fresh fish worth $14.3 million. In the years before independence, over 13,000 people were employed in the fishing industry. The Portuguese fleet in Angola consisted of slightly more than 800 boats, most of them fairly old but serviceable.

When colonial rule came to an end in 1975, the departing Portuguese took away most of their boats as well as their expertise on how and where to fish. In addition, many of the fish-processing and canning plants in Namibe were destroyed by their owners. The new MPLA government took over those enterprises largely abandoned by foreigners and quickly signed a series of agreements (notably with the Soviet Union, Spain, and Italy) to allow their state-run industries or private companies to fish the waters off Angola's coast in exchange for a share of the catch, usually about 40 percent. Foreign fleets reportedly caught more than 200,000 metric tons of fish in 1981; by 1985, output had risen to 403,500 metric tons, but dropped to 373,300 in 1986 and 295,700 in 1987. Four years later the figure stood at only 93,000 tons. Agreements remain with various European Union countries and Japan.

A major problem for Angola in connection with these agreements has been its inability to monitor the hauls of the foreign trawlers. With no means of direct verification, Luanda has had to rely on figures supplied by the contractors. It is widely believed that the amount of fish received by the government has been much less than specified. Other West African nations have attempted to solve this problem by having government representatives accompany each foreign trawler operating in its territorial waters or by operating navy coastal patrols.

Another concern is that foreign fishing fleets have been damaging the future productivity of the region by fishing illegally and using practices such as sucking techniques that destroy seashore plankton. Prior to the 1991 signing of a new Soviet-Angolan fishing protocol, many questions were raised about the 15 years of destructive fishing tactics practiced by the Soviets at the expense of Angola's fishing resources. As a consequence, a revised protocol called for a lower catch quota for the Commonwealth of Independent States (CIS). Whereas in 1990 the quota was 124,000 tons, of which Angola received one-third, the August 1991-July 1992 protocol limited the catch to 80,000 tons. The fishing protocol remained unaffected by the changes under way in the Soviet Union at the time of the signing.

Anticipating the potential of this sector, the government in 1980 began a program to expand domestic production with external help. Several countries began assisting in the rehabilitation of the fishing industry. In 1981, only 87 of the country's 263 trawlers were operational. The governments of Spain and Italy sold Angola 72 trawlers; the Italian government donated an additional 12 boats worth $5 million; the Arab Bank for Economic Development in Africa (BADEA) contributed three fishing boats and in 1981 granted a $10 million loan for fishing-industry rehabilitation; and the European Union made a substantial grant in 1984 to assist this sector. By 1987, the national fishing fleet numbered 466.

The Swedish Authority for International Development is financing salaries, extension of technical assistance, and the purchase of various pieces of equipment essential to the functioning of the Center for Professional Fisheries Training (CEFOPESCAS). Since its founding in 1982, CEFOPESCAS has graduated 424 basic technicians trained for various specialties in the fishing sector.

There is increasing interest on the part of other countries in developing both the fishing and canning industries within

Angola. A U.S. company, Mampeza International, has been producing canned fish since the early 1970s near Benguela and is in the process of expanding its operations. In fact, during the height of the war with UNITA before the signing of the Bicesse Peace Accords, the company's largest customer was the government, which bought Mampeza's product for its military forces. And even when UNITA forces overran much of Benguela province in the fighting that resumed after the 1992 elections, Mampeza continued its profitable operations.

Spain, Italy, and Norway, among others, have become involved in rebuilding canning and marketing operations in Namibe in the last few years. In 1988, an agreement was signed with the Soviet Union to construct a new fishing port in Namibe. Frozen fish is exported to Egypt and Nigeria, and Congo is allowed to haul 10,000 metric tons annually from Angolan waters in exchange for a share of the catch. By the late 1980s, Angola was collecting $3.7 million annually in foreign exchange from exports of fish and from license fees paid by foreign fleets.

Despite all these initiatives, the total fish catch is still only one-fourth of the 1972 amount. The challenges to be faced in the years ahead include the following:

- policing the amount of fish taken from Angolan waters to prevent depletion and to ensure that the government receives its proper percentage of the catch,
- guaranteeing that Angolans are enabled to compete with the foreign trawlers,
- increasing the percentage of the fish caught in Angolan territorial waters that is processed in-country rather than on foreign ships offshore, and
- ensuring the viability of artisanal (small-scale) fishing.

Overall, the fishing industry is one sector of the economy that has a good chance of recovery because of continuing foreign interest, especially from Spain, Italy, Portugal, the CIS, and Japan.

Tuna and shellfish harvesting are two aspects of fishing that could yield larger profits than those generated by current commercial operations in Angolan waters, but the full development of these subsectors would require investment from abroad. In this connection, it is encouraging to note that in 1991 an agreement was negotiated under whose terms Portuguese fishermen would export shellfish from Cuanza Sul province and harvest tuna from Angolan waters for processing on Japanese refrigerator ships and export to Japan. An Angolan-Spanish joint venture based in the port city of Tombwa also began exporting lobsters in 1993.

In addition, Italy, Portugal, and the Benguela provincial government have recently financed various centers for the support of small-scale artisanal fishing along the Angolan coast, specifically south of the Cuanza river in the areas of Cuanza Sul, Benguela, and Namibe. These fishery support centers are meant to provide fishermen with assistance in the repair and docking of their boats, as well as the preservation of fish.

The fishing sector of the economy has perhaps suffered the least since Angola returned to war. Its prospects for overall rehabilitation are strong given the extensive interest of outside actors in investing in both short-term projects and longer-term development efforts.

7

Diamonds

Until 1975, Angola was the fourth largest producer of diamonds in the world; just prior to the September 1992 elections it was the seventh largest in terms of annual dollar value. Mining is currently conducted in the northeastern part of the country near the border with Zaire in Lunda Norte and Lunda Sul provinces.

Diamonds have been found in three types of deposits in Angola: in gravel near rivers, in conglomerates called colonda, and in untapped volcanic pipes called kimberlites. Although data on proven reserves of the first two categories are unreliable (because detailed records were not passed on to successive holders of mining contracts), known reserves in Angola's six discovered kimberlite pipes, which are among the 10 largest in the world, have been proven at 180 million carats. If world diamond prices were to remain constant, and the kimberlites produce an average amount of gem-quality diamonds, the kimberlite reserves alone would be worth several billion dollars.

Five years after the discovery of alluvial diamonds in 1912, the Portuguese colonial government established the Companhia de Diamantes de Angola (DIAMANG). The Société Générale de Belgique (SGB), Ryan-Guggenheim, and an amalgamation of Portuguese and French banks were the principal financial supporters of DIAMANG. By the early 1970s, more than 2 million carats of diamonds were being produced annually in 42 separate areas, representing the third largest source of revenue for the government after oil and coffee. In 1971, DIAMANG's concession was limited to 50,000 square miles in Lunda Norte province. The Consorcio Mineiro de Diamantes (CONDIAMA)—consisting of the state, DIAMANG, and South African-based De Beers—was granted a concession for the remainder of Angola. In 1971, production peaked at 2.4 million carats.

Along with the rest of the economy, the diamond industry fared poorly during the transition to independence. DIAMANG's labor force fell from 20,000 to 6,000 following the withdrawal of Portuguese laborers in 1975. The new MPLA government took over the 38 percent of DIAMANG that had been controlled by the Portuguese government, and the nationalization of many small shareholders in 1977 and 1979 increased its share to 77.21 percent. The two other remaining major shareholders were SGB with 11.49 percent and its 54-percent subsidiary SIBEKA with 5.95 percent. The government contracted a subsidiary of De Beers to market Angolan diamonds via the Central Selling Organization (CSO) in London when output dropped to a mere 333,000 carats in 1977. The government also contracted with another subsidiary of De Beers (Mining and Technical Services Ltd. [MATS]) to improve production. Production reached 669,000 carats in 1979 and rose to a post-independence high of almost 1.5 million carats in 1980. Due to increased world prices, the 1980 output brought almost $230 million into state coffers.

Attacks on mines and transport routes by UNITA military forces, kidnapping of expatriate workers, and smuggling resulted in another steep decline in recorded diamond production during the1980s. Indeed, the war led to a virtual shutdown of the rich Cuango river valley region from 1984 to 1986 and the cessation of all overland transport to the Lunda provinces. All transport had to be done by air. Production fell to 714,000 carats in 1985 and 266,000 carats in 1986. Market fluctuations, combined with the production drop, resulted in a revenue decrease from $221 million in 1981 to $33 million in 1986. UNITA's President Jonas Savimbi has publicly admitted on several occasions that his organization derived a significant share of its resources between 1975 and 1991 from the sale of diamonds captured in military operations or mined in northeastern Angola (there have been widely circulated reports that a Belgian gemologist worked with UNITA and trained a cadre in diamond sorting).

In 1985, the MPLA government decided not to renew its contract with the CSO and MATS. DIAMANG was liquidated in 1986 because of operating losses; its functions were taken over by the state diamond company, Empresa Nacional de Diamantes de Angola (ENDIAMA), which began marketing directly to cutters.

In 1987, after ENDIAMA granted Roan Selection Trust International (RST International) a concession to begin mining in the Cuango (Kafunfo) region and another to the Sociedade Portuguesa de Empreendimentos (SPE) to operate in Lucapa under a two-year production-sharing contract, total output rose to over 750,000 carats, earning around $90 million. ENDIAMA also began mining in N'Zagi. In December of that year, an agreement was signed with the Soviet Union to cooperate in the mining of diamonds in as-yet-unspecified regions. In early 1991, a Brazilian holding company, Norberto Odebrecht, was awarded a seven-year contract to construct various diamond production facilities at Luzamba in northeastern Angola.

The marketing of Angolan diamonds became a competitive business in the late 1980s. Lazare Kaplan International agreed in March 1989 to market $20 million worth of uncut diamonds from ENDIAMA. ENDIAMA has also signed an agreement with Stevan Evens Diamonds to market diamonds from the Andrada and Lucapa production areas in Luanda Norte. This joint venture, based in Antwerp, is known as ENDIAMA Selling Corporation. A 1989 "declaration of intent" agreement with De Beers calling for expansion of local diamond production was solidified the following year when that company signed an agreement to provide a $50 million loan to ENDIAMA. The loan was earmarked for the development of the alluvial production in the Cuango river valley and the construction of a sorting and evaluation center in Luanda. ENDIAMA's contribution in this venture was to market the output from the Cuango area (which accounted for 77 percent of Angolan output in 1991) through the CSO. De Beers also agreed to spend $50 million over five years to develop one of Angola's kimberlite deposits. SIBEKA and the Russian government have also indicated interest in prospecting in northeastern Angola for kimberlite deposits.

In 1990, De Beers, which controls 80 percent of the world diamond trade and much of Angola's diamond exports, earned $230 million from the sale of 1.3 million carats from Angola. Over 90 percent of that output was gem quality (the most valuable grade).

The extraordinary benefits that can be realized in the diamond sector, under conditions of peace, can be seen in the dramatic rise in production during the first 10 months of 1992. Insiders estimate that the total value of diamonds that left Angola in that year prior to the resumption of war in mid-October was $750 million. Output slumped significantly in early 1993, with ENDIAMA reporting production at only 20,000 carats per month as compared to over 100,000 carats a year earlier.

The diamond industry faces a serious smuggling problem that has escalated in recent years. Even before the 1991 cease-fire, some employees of ENDIAMA (which is responsible for security in the diamond sector) reportedly stole diamonds to pay for consumer goods. These diamonds were in turn sold on the open market in Zaire or Portugal. After the 1991 peace agreement, the pace of freelance exploitation of the country's Cuango alluvial diamond reserves skyrocketed. As many as 40,000 prospectors (known in Portuguese as *garimpeiros*) pursued illegal fortunes in an area termed by some Angola's "Wild West" because of the lawless, violent culture that had developed there. During the first 10 months of 1992, De Beers was forced to purchase almost $250 million of illegally mined Angolan diamonds that turned up in Antwerp lest they reach the open market and drive down the international price. Overall illegal output between the signing of the peace agreement and the resumption of war reportedly averaged $25 million per month. The renewed civil war has slowed this process to roughly 10 percent of what it was during the interlude of peace.

The rapid occupation by UNITA forces of the diamond producing regions in the Cuango valley and Luzamba after the country returned to war in late 1992 forced both Odebrecht and RST to temporarily withdraw from their operations. UNITA steadily expanded its command of the two Lunda provinces in an effort to control the flow of diamonds. UNITA reportedly no longer mines its own diamonds, but instead buys them from illegal prospectors at prices well below market value and resells them in Europe.

If peace is achieved, ENDIAMA could look forward to regaining an estimated $30 to $50 million in annual revenues heretofore diverted to financing the military and could expect a drastic reduction in its air transportation costs. (During the lull in fighting after the 1991 cease-fire, ENDIAMA was able to save $25 million per year by returning to less-expensive ground transportation.) The companies having contracts with the government would be able to return and resume production. It is estimated that on the basis of existing mine development plans only, and assuming peaceful conditions, official output of diamonds would rise from around 900,000 carats in 1992 to 1.6 million carats in 1996. In addition, numerous firms have expressed an interest in mining for diamonds in other parts of the country.

Because the kimberlite-related initiatives are extremely costly and probably will not yield results for several years, mining for alluvial diamonds will remain in the short run the only significantly productive sector of the Angolan diamond industry. Alluvial reserves are estimated at between 40 million and 130 million carats. For these reasons, the Angolan government will quickly move to reassert its authority over the Lunda provinces following the signing of a peace accord.

Long-term prospects reside in the kimberlite deposits, however. In a 1987 economic agreement, the Soviet Union agreed to produce a detailed geological map of Angola but failed to do so. Such a map is of critical importance to the development of both undiscovered alluvial and kimberlite deposits. It is probable that there are more than the six kimberlite formations known to exist in Angola. The cost to produce a single one of these could be $1 billion.

8
Other Minerals

Deposits of more than 30 minerals are known to exist in Angola, including diamonds (discussed in the previous chapter), iron ore, uranium, gold, copper, titanium, chromium, phosphates, kaolin, manganese, bauxite, and coal. Of these, only iron ore and diamonds have been mined on any significant scale. Future production depends upon what can be done to deal with the following costly deterrents: (1) extensive war-related damage to the transport infrastructure (including roads, bridges, and railroads), (2) the lack of modern mining equipment, and (3) an acute shortage of trained artisans and managers to operate the mines.

Pre-independence interest in mineral production was substantial. By 1959, 240 mining and exploration concessions had been granted, of which 10 percent were involved in extraction.

Iron Ore

Before independence Angola's fourth most important export was iron ore. The Portuguese-owned Companhia Mineira do Lobito began mining iron ore at Cassinga in 1954. Production was slow in the early years, reaching only 106,000 tons in 1957. A decade later, reserves of ore with 63 percent iron content were proven at 130 million tons and an additional 1 billion tons was identified with iron contents ranging from 35 to 53 percent.

Portugal, in conjunction with West Germany's Krupp, invested $93 million to construct an additional 94-kilometer link on the Moçâmedes railroad connecting the Cassinga mines to ocean ports. This joint undertaking included the construction of an additional pier at Moçâmedes (now Namibe) to berth ships as large as 160,000 tons, and facilities to load 5,000 tons of iron ore per hour. Production at Cassinga remained steady at between 5 and 6 million tons per year from 1967 to 1974. Most of the prime-grade ore was extracted during this period. Following the 1974 overthrow of the Portuguese dictatorship by the Armed Forces Movement, the new Portuguese government decided to close down the mine before independence.

As with most of the other sectors of the economy, the major hindrance to expanding the production of minerals since the mid-1970s has been the prolonged civil war. Prospecting had come to a standstill by 1975 and the few operable transportation routes were intermittently attacked or destroyed by UNITA. In 1977 the iron ore mines were nationalized under the state enterprise Empresa Nacional de Ferro de Angola (FERRANGOL).

In 1979, FERRANGOL authorized a study on the viability of reopening the Cassinga mine. In 1981, the government accepted the recommendation of Austromineral, a subsidiary of Voest-Alpine, that the mine be rehabilitated with the objective of achieving an annual production rate of 1.1 million tons. The government's plans were disrupted, however, by UNITA attacks on the railroad linking the mine to Namibe and destruction of the mine's power plant. Although rehabilitation of Cassinga was eventually completed in 1986, it was not reopened, due primarily to the military situation, but also because the world market price for iron had declined to a point where production was no longer profitable. Another difficulty was that both the railroad and port in the town of Namibe would have required costly reconstruction in order to be usable for the transport and export of iron.

Also due to depressed market prices, deposits of 92 million tons of 32 percent iron ore found in Kassala-Kiturgo by a 1979 feasibility study have not been developed.

Prior to the September 1992 elections, several companies (including Japan's Mitsubishi, Mitsui, and Nissho Iwai; South Africa's Anglo American and ISCOR; and Great Britain's RTZ) expressed interest in Angola's iron ore deposits.

Phosphates

The state-operated phosphate company, FOSFANG, estimates that reserves of this mineral in Cabinda alone total more than 100 million tons. A consortium of Portuguese, British, and U.S. companies spent over $1 million prospecting in Cabinda following independence, but were forced to stop when their concession was withdrawn due to poor results and depleted financial resources.

An additional 50 million tons are believed to exist at Kindonacaxa (Kindonakasi) in Zaire province, although only 10 million tons have been proven. A program developed by the government in 1981 to produce 15,000 tons per year was subsequently canceled because war conditions precluded safe transport of the phosphates from the mine. Tests show that phosphates from this site are of sufficient quality to be used as fertilizers. By early 1994, the African Development Bank (ADB) had prepared an assessment to grant $1 million for an inventory of these reserves.

Other Minerals

Granite, marble, and quartz are currently being quarried in Namibe and Huíla provinces in southwestern Angola.

Angolan marble (white, pink, and other colors) has export potential but is more suitable for local markets because it is of lower quality once cut and polished. Angolan black granite is world renowned and in high demand in the United States and Japan. It is used mainly for tombstone production and sells for up to $500 per ton, giving it great market potential. The state-run ROREMINA (Empresa Nacional de Rochas Ornamentais) estimates that an initial investment of $2.5 million in granite quarrying will yield $3 million annually. A joint venture company known as RORANGOL was established with the Portuguese company Marmida to pursue this investment. A second agreement was reached with another Portuguese firm (SPE) under the joint venture title of ANGOROCHAS. The latter received a $3.8 million loan from the European Investment Bank to quarry black granite. A number of black granite quarries were operating in the southern part of the country before rail and road transportation to the port of Namibe became unreliable.

Although resources appear to be substantial in Cuanza Sul province, quartz production was held to a minimum because of the war, with only 301 tons worth $336,000 produced in 1988. The government is interested in mining the country's reserves of crystalline quartz, for which there exists a ready market in Europe. The government has also invested $25 million to gauge the production potential of kaolin found in Huíla province. In fact, the ADB has earmarked $750,000 for a study of the region's kaolin deposits, which could yield 250,000 tons per year for more than 20 years.

Two gold deposits have been discovered in Huíla and near Cassinga and Lombige, but the amounts are believed to be small. At least minor reserves of copper, lead, and zinc are known to have existed in Alto Zambeze. Mercury has also been found in Angola.

In January 1992, a new law on mining gave foreign investors wide-ranging rights and restricted state controls to regulatory functions. In the following month, a World Bank mission to Angola applauded the government's action but warned that the vaguely worded law risked making Angola uncompetitive in comparison with other countries. They recommended establishing a detailed mining code and an internationally competitive fiscal regime. The government's Secretariat of State for Geology and Mines agreed to undertake a comparative analysis of terms and conditions offered by other countries, but the war cut this process short.

The resumption of war has curtailed all projects and short-term prospects in the mining sector, but it is clear that in an era of peace, Angola's mining sector will offer a range of opportunities.

9
Oil

The second largest producer of oil in sub-Saharan Africa after Nigeria, Angola continues to find new reserves more quickly than it depletes existing ones. Proven recoverable reserves of Angolan crude are currently estimated at over 3 billion barrels and daily production stands at slightly more than 500,000 barrels. This single sector stands out as the only one to post overall growth since independence; it still has significant potential.

Exploration for Angolan oil began in 1910, but did not yield any tangible results until 1955, when an onshore discovery was made by Petrofina at the Benfica field near Luanda. Subsequently, Gulf Oil Company, through its subsidiary Cabinda Gulf Oil Company (CABGOC), began prospecting in the northern enclave of Cabinda. In 1966, CABGOC tapped a major offshore field at Malongo that held reserves far beyond those found onshore. By 1969, overall production stood at 49,000 barrels per day (b/d). By 1973, when production had risen to 163,000 b/d, oil had overtaken coffee as Angola's largest revenue-generating export.

In 1975 and early 1976, output plummeted when the civil war forced CABGOC's temporary evacuation from operations in Cabinda. Although CABGOC returned in mid-1976, it was cautious about investing in exploration because the MPLA government was slow in setting an agenda for the oil sector. Production stood at 171,000 b/d in 1977, but steadily decreased over the following five years to 130,000 in 1982.

Initial steps to develop a national oil policy began with the formation of the Sociedade Nacional de Combustiveis de Angola (SONANGOL) in 1976. Given responsibility to coordinate and control petroleum production within the country, SONANGOL took control of the assets and operations of ANGOL, the Portuguese oil subsidiary, in 1977. In the following year a law was enacted designating SONANGOL as the exclusive concessionaire for all oil exploration and production rights. The 1978 statute permitted foreign oil companies to operate in Angola either under a production-sharing agreement or on a joint-venture basis with the national oil company.

Under the terms of a set of production-sharing agreements negotiated by SONANGOL, foreign companies are required to pay for the development of each offshore site in exchange for a share of the oil produced. Each company must also pay a tax on that oil to the government. In joint ventures, SONANGOL and its partners divide exploration and production costs, as well as any petroleum produced. SONANGOL mandated for itself a 51 percent stake in joint-venture operations such as those operated by CABGOC, Petrofina, Texaco, and Elf Aquitaine.

A seismic survey of the continental shelf off Angola's coast undertaken by SONANGOL in 1978-1979 led to the division of the entire Angolan coastal area into 13 blocks (about 4,000 square kilometers each) as organized areas for oil exploration. An additional 17 blocks were subsequently delineated in areas of deeper water farther offshore but adjacent to the original 13. The Cabinda concession was divided into three offshore areas (known as A, B, and C) and three unexplored onshore areas (known as Cabinda North, Cabinda Central, and Cabinda South). Due to renegotiation and lapsing contracts, some of the blocks south of the Cabinda concession have also been subdivided.

Oil companies have been attracted to Angola by low operating costs, the high probability of new discoveries (65 percent success rate for 1987-1991, compared to only 22 percent in the North Sea), and the favorable business climate offered by SONANGOL. At least 15 foreign companies, including Chevron (which acquired Gulf Oil in 1984), Petrofina, Texaco, Elf Aquitaine, Conoco, Agip, and Petrobrás, were involved in oil exploration as of 1991. Total foreign investment in exploration and production off Angola's coast from 1980 to 1986 was $2.7 billion. An additional $2 billion was invested in exploration and development from 1987 to 1990. The figure for 1993-1997 is expected to reach $4 billion, primarily due to the high-risk, high-cost nature of operations in the deep-water blocks 14 to 17 far off the northwest coast.

A monthly analysis of crude oil production from 1988 through mid-1990 shows that output remained between 439,210 and slightly more than 500,000 b/d. Half of the annual output comes from Cabinda. Average production from this area in 1990 was about 250,000 b/d, of which more than two-thirds came from the massive Takula field. The Takula field's output is expected to rise following the recent investment of $200 million in a water-injection project. An additional $230 million has been invested in the Numbi field to realize its potential. Production in Cabinda was 311,000 b/d in 1992 and is expected to increase to 380,000 b/d by 1997. CABGOC (block operator) has a 39.2 percent interest in Cabinda blocks A, B, and C, compared to SONANGOL's 41 percent, Elf Aquitaine's 10 percent, and Agip's 9.8 percent.

Near the mouth of the Zaire river, Block 2 is subdivided into areas 2/92 (which is under exploration and operated by Total [60 percent] with SONANGOL [40 percent]) and 2/85 (under production and operated by Texaco [20 percent] with Total [27.5 percent], Petrobrás [27.5 percent], and SONANGOL [25 percent]). Block 2 has also seen increases in exploration and production, including the drilling of 34 development wells since 1987. By mid-1989, production in the entire block had risen to nearly 35,000 b/d and as of 1991 the output reached 48,000 b/d. Production the following year was estimated at 58,000 b/d. This figure is expected to increase further once the Mavanga field comes into production. Three new finds with estimated reserves of 7.5 million barrels prompted Petrobrás to invest another $50 million in Block 2 before the end of 1991.

Block 3, located off N'Zeto, one of Angola's northernmost coastal towns, has surprised many oil analysts by the rapidity of its production growth. It is subdivided three ways. Areas 3/85 and 3/91 are jointly operated by Elf Aquitaine (50 percent), Agip (15 percent), AJOCO (12.5 percent), Repsol (6.25 percent), Svenska (6.25 percent), and INA Naftaplin and INA Naftagas (each with 5 percent). Elf Aquitaine (50 percent) serves as operator in area 3/80; the other partners are AJOCO (25 percent), Agip (15 percent), and INA Naftaplin and INA Naftagas (each with 5 percent). Elf Aquitaine began exploration here with operating rights in the early 1980s, and by the time its fields came on line in 1986, Block 3 accounted for almost 18 percent of Angola's total output. Investments from 1987 to 1990 totaled $700 million and production rose from an average of 110,000 b/d in 1988 to 120,000 b/d in 1989. In January 1992, crude oil production from this block reached 170,000 b/d.

The following is a summary of activity in the remaining blocks:

- Onshore Cabinda North (CN) is under the operatorship of Occidental (35 percent) with Teikoku (25 percent), Nisti Oy (20 percent), and SONANGOL (20 percent). Cabinda

Central (CC) operations are controlled by British Petroleum (26 percent) with Repsol (25 percent), Petrogal (20 percent), SONANGOL (20 percent), and Statoil (9 percent). Cabinda South (CS) is operated by Petrofina (45 percent), with the remainder to be negotiated but expected to be awarded to SONANGOL (20 percent), Elf Aquitaine (20 percent), and Anglo-Suisse (15 percent). Because of the government's ongoing war with two armed factions of the FLEC, none of the three areas are currently under active exploration.

- Block 1 was awarded in 1982 to Agip (operatorship and 50 percent), Elf Aquitaine (25 percent), Petrogal (10 percent), INA Naftagas (7.5 percent), and INA Naftaplin (7.5 percent). It has yielded little oil despite substantial investment over the years. (It had a minor discovery, Safueiro, which came onstream in 1991, at about 4,000 b/d.) Agip has reportedly relinquished its operatorship of this block with the exception of its one active well. According to reports, Shell-Pecten will become the operator (50 percent) with Maxus (25 percent) and Engen (25 percent).

- Block 4 (which had been explored earlier and abandoned) was awarded to Ranger Oil as operator (70 percent), with the remainder being held by SONANGOL (20 percent) and Heritage (10 percent). Under the three-year arrangement with SONANGOL, extendable for two more one-year terms, operations began in early 1992 with the creation of three exploration wells and the acquisition of seismic data. Because Block 4, directly south off the coast from N'Zeto, is next to a key producing area (Block 3), there is some reason to hope that it may contain significant oil reserves. A commercial discovery was made in 1993 with a well yielding 4,600 b/d. A second well will be drilled in early 1994 as part of a $20 million exploration program.

- Block 5, which is currently open, was operated by Conoco (50 percent) with Hispanoil, and Agip. A total of $37 million was invested in the initial three years of drilling, which began in 1987 but was abandoned in 1992.

- Block 6, directly offshore from Luanda, is operated by Conoco (15 percent) with Dupont (10 percent), Pecten (25 percent), Nippon Mining (20 percent), Total (15 percent), Eagle (15 percent), and Citizens Energy (option for 5 percent). This block had been explored previously by Total.

- The concession for Block 7, offshore just south of Luanda, was granted to Elf Aquitaine as operator in 1990. Under a contract that was signed in 1991, Elf Aquitaine negotiated a partnership with Norsk Hydro (13 percent), AJOCO (10 percent), OMV (10 percent), British Gas (7.5 percent), Enterprise (7.5 percent), and Petro Inett Corporation (7 percent). Elf Aquitaine has a 45 percent share. The initial wells drilled have produced no discoveries.

- A contract to operate in Block 8 (along Bengo and Cuanza Sul provinces) was awarded to a consortium consisting of Total as operator with 40 percent, Petrofina (40 percent), Britoil (10 percent), and Statoil (10 percent).

- Operatorship of Block 9, offshore from Cuanza Sul, was awarded to Texaco (50 percent) with OMV (25 percent), and Norsk Hydro (25 percent).

- Blocks 10 through 13 (off the coasts of Benguela and Namibe provinces) have yet to be parceled out.

- Two prime deep-water blocks off Cabinda (14 and 15) will be signed shortly. Block 14 will have Chevron as operator (31 percent), Agip (20 percent), Total (20 percent), SONANGOL (20 percent), and Petrogal (9 percent). Block 15 will see Exxon as operator (40 percent), British Petroleum (40 percent), and Agip (20 percent).

- It is likely that operatorship in Block 16 will be awarded to Shell (50 percent) with Texaco (15 percent), Exxon (15 percent), Elf Aquitaine (10 percent), and Petrofina (10 percent).

- Elf Aquitaine may also be chosen to operate Block 17 (50 percent) with Exxon (20 percent), Petrofina (15 percent), and Norsk Hydro (15 percent).

- The remaining Blocks 18 to 30 are open.

Most of the oil produced in Angola is shipped abroad for processing. The one significant refinery that meets most of Angola's requirements is located near Luanda and jointly owned by SONANGOL (which acquired a majority holding in 1986) and Petrofina. This facility (known as PETRANGOL), which had an input of 38,000 b/d in 1992, produces a range of products from jet fuel to domestic gas. The sale of excess production from the refinery earned Angola $93 million in 1985; this figure dropped to $39 million in 1986, but recovered to $53 million in 1991. SONANGOL distributes all oil products within the country. Mobil, which withdrew entirely during the 1980s, was the last independent distributor of oil products in Angola.

Prices for Angolan oil rose as high as $40 b/d at the height of the Gulf crisis in September and October 1990. This price escalation, coupled with increases in production (to over 500,000 b/d), resulted in dramatically increased earnings from the second quarter ($630 million) to the third ($1.07 billion).

In August 1991, the Petroleum Ministry began unsuccessful negotiations with South Africa's Strategic Fuel Fund on a deal to barter oil worth $600 million per year for foodstuffs and mining equipment. If this barter deal (which would have allowed South Africa to sell Angolan crude oil on the international spot market) had gone through, some analysts predicted that Angolan Takula crude might have replaced the Nigerian standard as the price benchmark for West African oil producers.

Estimates from the Ministry of Planning indicate that the petroleum sector accounted for 41.5 percent of total gross domestic product (GDP) by 1991. The rapid growth in this sector, along with the poor performance of the non-oil economy, has left Angola exceptionally vulnerable to oil shocks. Government finances have come to depend overwhelmingly on oil revenue. Oil taxes and revenues provided almost 49 percent of total revenue in 1991, and were projected to provide 79 percent of the total revenue in the 1992 budget. Until the mid-1980s, fast-rising oil income disguised the country's economic ill health. When world oil prices collapsed in 1986, however, Angola's balance of payments and the government budget lurched into large deficits. Oil export earnings were down 15 percent in 1993 due mainly to declining international oil prices.

The resumption of war following the September 1992 elections caused disruptions in Soyo at the mouth of the Congo river when UNITA took the city from the government in early 1993.

After the government recaptured the town, UNITA returned in May 1993 and appears to have firm control. After initially attempting to damage offshore oil rigs with mortar and artillery barrages, UNITA refrained from attacking such assets until November 1993, when its forces fired at a tanker offshore. Onshore production by Petrofina has ceased, but Texaco resumed its offshore output in August 1993. Military activities in Soyo cut Angolan daily production 6 percent in 1993.

Exploration of onshore regions in Cabinda is also inhibited by the activities of two armed FLEC factions. The drive for Cabindan independence, whose roots go back to the 1960s, will require its own negotiated solution. Thus far, however, the factions have not seriously interrupted offshore production in Cabinda.

Despite the resumption of war, the petroleum sector is set for steady production increases throughout the 1990s. Angola's output in 2000 has been estimated at 700,000 b/d. The normally constructive business approach of the Angolan government, favorable geology, and low operating costs continue to attract a variety of oil companies. Angola has the additional benefit of not being a member of the Organization of Petroleum Exporting Countries (OPEC), so that it is not limited by production quotas. Perhaps the greatest potential for increased production lies in Angola's deep-water acreage. Initial geological studies show that potential reserves in Blocks 14 to 17 could double current proven reserves of some 3 billion barrels.

10

Hydroelectric Power

Angola possesses enormous hydroelectric potential. A number of large and powerful rivers cross the country, including the Cunene, Cubango, Cuanza, and Cuango. Dams have been built in each of the three electrification grids (northern, central, and southern) constructed by the Portuguese and South Africans before independence.

Present electric generating capacity far exceeds the country's needs. In 1987, for example, hydroelectric capacity was 771 GWh, but consumption was only 142 GWh. By the year 2000, when maximum electricity output is expected to reach 2,400 GWh, the projected demand is now assessed at only 439 GWh.

The following hydroelectric dams are currently in operation:

- The Cambambe dam on the Cuanza river, which provides most of the electricity for Luanda and surrounding areas, produces the same amount of power today (370 KWh) as it did in 1972. Although it would be relatively easy to double its capacity, current demand does not justify such a move. The Mabubas dam on the Dande river also supplies Luanda with electricity.

- The Lobito-Benguela area is supplied with power from the Biopio dam. A dam at Lomaum, on the Catumbela river, also supplied this area with power prior to being severely damaged during the civil war.

- The Gove dam on the Cunene river was completed (with South African capital) before independence. Built to provide electricity for Huambo, it has not been functional since 1986, when UNITA successfully sabotaged the control equipment. A later attack threatened to destroy the dam itself.

- Farther south, the Matala dam on the Cunene river supplies electricity to Namibe, Lubango, and Cassinga.

- Along the Namibian border, the Ruacana and Calueque dams provide electricity and irrigation for northern Namibia. Once transmission facilities are constructed, they will be able to provide low-cost power for the Tsumeb mines, Walvis Bay, and Windhoek.

In addition to these existing hydroelectric facilities, the unfinished Capanda complex in Malanje province is expected to increase Angola's generating capacity by almost 100 percent and generate enough power to meet the country's needs through at least 2030. A Brazilian firm, Norberto Odebrecht, has been supervising construction of the dam and has provided specialized personnel via a contract with Furnas Centrais Electrias, a firm owned by the Brazilian government. In 1992, over 2,200 Angolans comprised 63 percent of the total work force, while 536 Brazilians filled many of the project's engineering positions.

The total estimated cost of the dam is $2 billion. Banco do Brasil has arranged loans worth $690 million for the dam's construction. The Soviet Union (and now the Russian state) is financing up to $275 million and standby credits through its state-owned Technopromoexport. The Soviets completed work on the hydrology, geology, and topography of the dam area. Soviet turbine equipment was due to be mounted in early October 1991 with the completed construction of 70 percent of the dam, but there were delays due to the changes taking place in the former Soviet Union. Following the resumption of war in October 1992, construction on the nearly completed complex was halted and all expatriate workers withdrawn from the site.

According to the World Bank, there is no present or near-term need for a dam such as the one under construction at Capanda because the country's poor power transmission and distribution facilities limit the utility of the electricity it will generate. Moreover, the project has increased the nation's debt by an estimated $500 million. The World Bank and the United Nations Development Program (UNDP) have strongly counseled against its construction, terming the facility a "prestige project," and have drafted an alternative $215 million prospectus for reconstruction and restoration of the existing electrical system.

Capanda will prove important, however, in the longer run after peace returns to Angola. Situated in the northern grid,

Capanda will be a ready source of energy for the manufacturing, transport, and other commercial sectors of the economy. The realization of this significant potential will depend on the government's ability to greatly expand the electrical grid in this region and to provide service to an ever-increasing populace.

As part of its effort to reduce dependence on South Africa, Namibia has arranged to build a new power station at Epupa in return for an Angolan pledge to repair the Gove and Calueque dams on the Cunene river. France's Caisse Centrale de Coopération Économique announced a loan in August 1990 for rehabilitating the diesel power stations in Lobito and Namibe, which currently supply these cities with power. A Portuguese consortium has already undertaken a $40 million rehabilitation effort on the Lomaum dam. The governments of Spain and Italy have also provided assistance in this sector.

Large sums of money will have to be spent to modernize and rebuild the country's electrical infrastructure. Providing electricity to all parts of the country is too costly to be feasible in the near term. Initially, it will be necessary to concentrate on revitalizing the existing power grids serving urban areas. All have been attacked by UNITA during various stages of the war in addition to the destruction of electrical pylons. The Portuguese government invested over $150 million in the rehabilitation of the Lomaum dam and East Germany granted $100 million in the 1980s for various projects including improving hydroelectric facilities near Luanda.

The vast energy potential of Angola as a whole has made Luanda the seat of the SADC regional grouping's Energy Sector Technical and Administrative Unit. Angola is likely to replace South Africa as the region's main energy supplier in the post-conflict era.

11

Manufacturing

The number of Portuguese settlers in Angola rose from 44,000 immediately following World War II to nearly 350,000 by 1974. This influx brought an increasing demand for consumer goods and the human resources to develop and operate Angola's nascent manufacturing sector. Following the onset of nationalist uprisings in 1961, Lisbon offered generous incentives to its overseas settlers not only to maintain their fledgling operations, but to reinvest and expand. The Portuguese government also enacted a series of import restriction laws encouraging the production of goods in the overseas territories. Between 1962 and 1970, annual growth in Angola's manufacturing output averaged 19 percent and the variety of items being produced continually expanded. By the early 1970s, the range of import-substitution products included beer, pasta, cloth, paint, cars, tires, steel, and many other items. By 1974, almost 4,000 manufacturing enterprises were in operation, employing more than 200,000 people and producing $650 million in goods annually that accounted for 16 percent of GDP.

Following Angola's sudden transition to independence in 1975, the fleeing Portuguese settlers destroyed or abandoned most of the manufacturing facilities. By March 1976, only 280 of the enterprises remained in operation. The ensuing civil war and nationalization of 78 percent of the manufacturing sector (abandoned by the Portuguese) by the new MPLA government led to many additional problems, including shortages of raw materials, spare parts, and agricultural products; periodic disruptions of power and water service; and an increasingly inadequate internal distribution system for finished products.

By 1984, the number of persons employed in the manufacturing sector was 85,000—115,000 fewer than 10 years earlier. By 1990, however, the figure had risen to 120,000. Although production levels had returned to 54 percent of their 1973 amount by 1985, the steep decline in oil prices the following year reduced the foreign-exchange earnings necessary to import industrial raw materials. This led to drastic cuts in the manufacturing budget—from $200 million in 1985 to $69 million in 1986. As a result, over 90 percent of the country's finished manufactured-goods needs now must be met by imports.

Although most of the manufacturing enterprises were based in coastal cities, the war nevertheless affected their ability to operate. Disruptions in the agricultural and transport sectors seriously affected the supply of domestic raw materials. Valuable foreign exchange had to be spent on imports, which were often diverted from the ports to the parallel markets. Even when finished goods could be produced by Angolan factories, the war made it difficult to deliver them to potential consumers inside the country.

In addition, a burdensome state bureaucracy, price controls, and unreliable supplies of electricity and water all had a negative impact on this important sector.

There are three principal subsectors in the Angolan manufacturing industry: food processing, light industry, and heavy industry. The following is a summary of the growth potential of each of these subsectors.

Food Processing

The food, beverages, and tobacco subsector is the largest and most important division of the manufacturing industry. Both before and after independence, this subsector has been dominated by the production of a single item—beer. In 1973, some 120 million liters of beer were produced in Angola. The postindependence high of 78 million liters in 1979 was followed by a drop to 47 million liters in 1987. When beer unofficially replaced the kwanza (the Angolan monetary unit) as the currency of choice in the parallel market in the late 1980s and early 1990s, the growth potential of this product was recognized.

In the pre-independence era, hundreds of facilities were established to process domestically produced agricultural derivatives—notably beer, soft drinks, sugar, wheat flour, pasta, cooking oil, molasses, and salt. Indeed, this subsector produced 34 percent of the total output in the manufacturing sector in 1987 (see table 11.1).

Each product in the food processing industry has the potential for expanded production. Certain products have benefited from government efforts to boost output to maintain functional

Table 11.1
Food-Processing Production

Product	Unit	1973	1979	1987	1991
Beer	mn. liters	120	78	47	48
Soft drinks	mn. liters	49	23	7	6
Sugar	ton	80,909	31,843	15,342	n.a.
Wheat flour	ton	82,925	47,581	31,730	19,000
Pasta	ton	8,678	4,704	3,603	n.a.
Cooking oil	kl	14,464	4,074	4,490	2,300
Molasses	ton	37,252	12,171	6,904	n.a.
Salt	ton	96,757	23,008	3,746	6,600

Source: UNDP/WB Report No. 7283–ANG, p. 360 and *Angola to 2000*, p. 129.

dietary levels, but others have not received adequate capital and technological inputs. Public-sector investment in the food-processing subsector amounted to $5 million in 1980, $23 million in both 1981 and 1982, and $8 million in 1986 (the next recorded date). In 1985, this subsector was producing only 37 percent of its 1973 output.

Assuming a rebirth of the agricultural and transport sectors and the establishment of an uncumbersome state bureaucracy in a post-conflict era, the food-processing subsector could witness a revival to pre-independence production levels within a matter of years. An infusion of capital, technology, and training would, of course, be a prerequisite.

Light Industry

The light industry subsector achieved 62 percent of its 1973 production in 1987; most of the output was in the form of cloth (see table 11.2). In 1979, French industrialists constructed a textile factory in Benguela with a capacity of 16 million square meters of cloth per year. (This facility was destroyed by UNITA following the September 1992 elections.) In 1983, another textile factory, TEXTANG II (a parastatal, at present slated for privatization), began operations in Luanda with the ability to produce 18 million square meters of cloth per year. Production of other goods in this subsector—such as shoes, matches, soap, paint, plastic bottles, and glues—has fared poorly.

The potential for growth in this subsector is evident. Currently, the government must rely on imports to make up for inadequate local production of light industrial goods. Even with the introduction of the two previously cited textile factories, cloth production slackened during much of the 1980s because the drop in oil revenues made it difficult to import raw cotton. Government investment in this subsector stood at $5 million in 1980, rose to $44 million the following year, leveled off at about $33 million in 1982, and was reported to be $10 million in 1986. The European Investment Bank and the French government have extended $15 million in low-interest loans to rebuild unspecified projects in this subsector.

In mid-1987, the African Development Bank approved a loan for the construction of three pharmaceutical plants by a Luso-Belgian consortium. These plants, completed in 1991, will manufacture over 60 pharmaceutical products in factories in Luanda and Benguela. In September 1990, Belgium announced that it

Table 11.2
Light Industry Production

Product	Unit	1973	1979	1987	1991
Cloth	1,000 m^2	17,975	11,532	5,919	5,600
Shoes	1,000 prs.	3,244	997	750	216
Matches	1,000 boxes	93,053	19,147	8,855	100
Soap	ton	17,582	8,454	2,204	4,700
Paint	ton	8,449	3,904	1,390	1,882
Plastic bottles	1,000s	13,326	1,426	1,103	n.a.
Glue	ton	455	513	104	254

Source: UNDP/WB Report No. 7823–ANG, p. 361 and Angola to 2000, p. 130.

would provide a $1 billion interest-free loan to Angola toward the production of essential medicines.

Heavy Industry

The heavy industry subsector accounts for roughly 15 percent of the total output in the manufacturing sector (see table 11.3). Most of the goods produced in this subsector, however, are not representative of the classic "heavy industry" category. Angolan factories in this subsector include a medium-sized steel facility, a cement plant, and the Luanda petroleum refinery. The government invested $11 million in heavy industry in 1980, $57 million in 1981, $13 million in 1982, and $11 million in 1986. During these years, this subsector experienced double-digit growth, especially in the areas of vehicle assembly, steel tubes, the assembly of radio and television sets, and the manufacture of tires.

A steel factory built in Luanda by the Portuguese in 1972-1973 was reopened in 1984. Although this facility has the capacity to produce 40,000 tons of steel and 60,000 tons of rods per year, its reopening has had little direct effect on steel rod output. A steel tubing plant that produced 14,309 tons in 1973 generated only 3,112 tons in 1986. A total of 3,758 tons of zinc sheets (as compared to 12,009 tons in 1973) was produced in 1986 at a plant that is 50 percent owned by Japan's Mitsubishi. In 1984-1985, a construction facility was built in Ambriz with French assistance to manufacture such oil drilling equipment as platforms and jackets for offshore drilling sites. Owned by Bougys Offshore (90 percent) and the Angolan government (10 percent), the Ambriz site has been attacked twice by UNITA since the resumption of fighting in 1992. In September 1987, a combined Angolan-Dutch entity began to build trucks in Luanda with Dutch technical assistance. The manufacture of construction materials also began to bring substantial export earnings to the government prior to the resumption of war.

The heavy industry subsector will not fare well in the near future. An end to hostilities and adoption of economic reforms will soon bring to an end the state subsidies that keep many of these bloated companies afloat. Most of these organizations are unable to compete with international competitors and will rapidly lose market share in a situation of decreased state controls. The longer-term picture is brighter, however; government

Table 11.3
Heavy Industry Production

Product	Unit	1973	1979	1987	1991
Tires		191,000	108,651	12,480	20,300
Bicycles		36,518	8,750	13,750	6,000
Motorcycles		6,128	3,960	5,500	n.a.
Steel rods	ton	26,572	4,134	2,500	n.a.
Batteries		62,292	52,304	16,880	6,400
Oxygen	1,000 m^3	852	406	725	390
Radios		25,821	70,945	33,468	52,000
Machetes	1,000s	457	68	300	24

Source: UNDP/WB Report No. 7283–ANG, p. 362 and *Angola to 2000*, p. 131.

restructuring of this sector should ultimately produce more efficient firms that can play an important role in reconstructing the country's physical infrastructure in an era without war.

12

Transportation

Of all the sectors affected by war, transportation is perhaps the one that will take the longest to rebuild. Roads and railways were severely damaged and ports became antiquated and were forced to shift from export to import functions. If this sector's problems are not addressed on a priority basis following the restoration of peace, development of the economy as a whole will be extremely difficult.

Well aware of this situation, the World Bank in 1991 approved a nearly $38 million credit for an Infrastructure Rehabilitation Engineering Project that would bolster the development of an overall policy approach to this critical sector. The Bank committed an additional $41 million the following year for emergency rehabilitation purposes. The resumption of war has postponed any realization of the expected goals.

Roads

Angola has 72,323 kilometers of roads, of which 8,317 kilometers are paved. Major routes link Luanda to Uíge province in the north, to Moxico province in the east, and to Namibe province in the south. More than 60 percent of the paved roads are in need of substantial repair or replacement due to the war and lack of maintenance since independence. As with all modes of transportation in Angola, travel by land during the war was uncertain and dangerous because of the high incidence of sabotage by UNITA forces. Land mines often go undetected until they are detonated by a military or civilian vehicle. The destruction of scores of bridges has made it extremely difficult to reach many parts of the country.

The Ministry of Transport and Communications estimates that it could take from 10 to 15 years to restore Angola's existing roads to prewar status. In response, the government created the

National Highway Institute of Angola in 1990 to prepare for a rapid rehabilitation of the country's road system.

Although there were 30,000 trucks in the country by 1987, many are now inoperable. The Ministry of Transport and Communications (MINTEC) had prohibited the importation of vehicles for non-MINTEC uses, leaving the state sector with a modern fleet of trucks while the private sector relied on aging trucks to transport people and goods. One effect of the lack of operable vehicles is a constriction on the amount of products that can be shipped to various parts of the country. In 1985, slightly less than a million tons of goods were shipped via roads in Angola. The figure rose the following year to just over 1.3 million tons but fell back again in 1987 to just over 1 million. The number of passengers traveling by roads fell from over 29 million in 1985 to about 19 million in 1986 and slightly over 16 million in 1987.

Plans were developed for the rehabilitation of Angolan roads and passenger transportation systems following the signing of the May 1991 peace agreement. The continued lack of modern and efficient vehicles could preclude early expansion in commercial use of roads when the present fighting ends. Related problems indicate a critical shortage of trained mechanics, spare parts, and repair facilities. The establishment of a road maintenance organization also requires priority attention. After the 1991 cease-fire, the Ministry of Public Works and Urban Affairs said that the country needed to invest $150 million to rebuild bridges and repair 2,000 kilometers of asphalt roads. Independent estimates of the cost of repairing the country's road system run as high as $640 million.

Prior to the resumption of war, the main public transportation service was ETIM (Intermunicipal Transportation Enterprise), which ran through the provinces of Cuanza Norte, Malanje, and Uíge and the city of Saurimo. ETIM was established in 1980 but its services steadily diminished during the war as the number of its operational vehicles dropped from 48 to 22. Rehabilitation of these lines is one of the government's transportation priorities. According to a recent French study, the potential for mass transit in urban areas such as Luanda is extremely promising over the longer term.

Railroads

Almost 3,100 kilometers of track compose the country's three railways (a fourth line from Porto Amboim to Gabela in Cuanza

Railroads in Angola

Reprinted, by permission, from *Africa Review 1992*, Walden Publishing Ltd, England.

Sul province was abandoned in 1974). Each was constructed during the colonial era to transport minerals and natural resources from inland areas to ports for shipment abroad. All three were subjected to UNITA military attacks during the civil war; according to recent estimates, only 20 percent of the country's railway lines are operable on a normal basis; in terms of annual tonnage carried, the railroads are running at only 3 percent of their peak 1973 levels.

The Namibe railroad, linking this southern coastal city and Menongue (756 kilometers), was constructed by the Portuguese to transport iron ore from mines in Cuando Cubango province to the Atlantic coast. It also has two branches that run from Chiange to Lubango, and from Dongo to Cassinga. With the 1975 halt in mining due to the war, freight traffic on this line virtually ended; its primary use is now for passenger traffic. Until recently, the Namibe line ran only about as far as Matala (430 kilometers), operating under military escort.

When military hostilities finally end in Angola, the Namibe line is well located to provide transportation for potential agricultural and livestock development in the southeastern region of the country. There are, however, some problems to be resolved:

- freight wagons full of imports will run from the coast to inland areas, but will be empty on their return,
- the railroad suffers from an inadequate stock of 18 passenger carriages, 10 locomotives, and 273 freight wagons,
- for passengers, the ride is usually overcrowded and uncomfortable, and
- the railroad suffers from a severe lack of trained personnel among its staff of 1,700.

Recent estimates place the cost of rehabilitating the railroad and the port at $272 million.

The Luanda railroad, the northernmost of the three, used to link Luanda to Malanje, but 10 bridges between Dondo and Malanje were destroyed by UNITA prior to the signing of the May 1991 peace agreement, after which it operated only as far as Dondo (210 kilometers). Since the resumption of war following the elections, the line has ceased operations. Because this railroad is situated in the most densely populated region of the country, its potential passenger and cargo (especially agricultural products) traffic is enormous. In order to satisfy the area's unmet demand, however, the railway will need much more than its present 5 locomotives, 22 carriages, and 323 wagons. Prior to the resumption of war in late 1992, this line operated at 18 percent of peak capacity in terms of tonnage carried.

The Benguela, Angola's largest and best-known railroad, runs from Lobito through Benguela and across the central highlands of the country to Shaba province in southern Zaire and finally Zambia. Before its international role was put on hold by rebel attacks following independence, the Benguela line transported 50 percent of landlocked Zambia's and 90 percent of Zaire's imports and exports from and to the sea, including raw materials such as copper and zinc. Each of these countries must now rely on South African ports or less dependable routes through Mozambique or Tanzania.

In early 1975 the Cubal variant (a new 163-kilometer stretch designed to bypass steep gradients and outfitted with diesel locomotives to replace aging steam engines) began operation between Cubal and Benguela. The upgrades more than doubled the line's freight capacity to 5 million tons, but military clashes in late 1975 put the line out of operation. Service was reopened into Zaire in 1978, but UNITA attacks limited traffic to a trickle. Service past Huambo was truncated in 1982 following a determined effort by UNITA to shut the railroad down.

With 4,500 employees, the Benguela operates 18 locomotives, 26 passenger carriages, and 1,528 cargo wagons. As with the other two railroads in Angola, the staff is undertrained and the amount of equipment is insufficient. A railroad repair and training school operates in Huambo, and a diesel locomotive repair facility is currently under construction.

The MPLA government announced on June 22, 1991 that commercial operations of the Benguela railway would soon resume. In November of that year, service (intermittent and hampered by frequent derailments) was restored from the coastal region to Huambo. Plans to expand service farther inland to Cuito were shelved because 37 bridges on the line heading east from Huambo had been destroyed. The resumption of war dashed all hopes of any further short-term rehabilitation effort and all inland transport along this line.

Rehabilitation of the Benguela railroad (which would cost an estimated $572 million) has become an important political and economic symbol in southern Africa. Tractebel, a subsidiary of the Belgian conglomerate Société Générale de Belgique (SGB), undertook to conduct a feasibility study of the entire length of the railroad in late 1991 (bridges, buildings, locomotives, railway cars, and telecommunications equipment). SGB controls 90 percent of the Benguela concession through Tanks Consolidated Investments, its subsidiary based in the Virgin Islands, and is interested in financing the Benguela rehabilitation project. The concession is due to expire in 2001, with the 1,100 kilometers of track returning at that time to the hands of the Angolan government (which currently owns the other 10 percent).

Rehabilitation of the Benguela will greatly increase Angola's economic potential. Safe and regular transport to and from the central highlands region of the country is essential to the expansion of agricultural, livestock, and timber production. A fully functional Benguela railroad would also provide the government with increased revenues (which would total an estimated $100 million annually) because of its importance as an alternate transport route to world markets for Zaire and Zambia, and because it would generate additional revenues for Benguela and Lobito harbors.

International donors (notably the European Union, Belgium, Portugal, and Italy) have already expressed concrete interest in a $90 million package of projects envisaged for its rehabilitation. The rebuilding of the railroad was also a prime objective of the SADC regional grouping when it last substantially addressed this issue in 1988. SADC proposed a $346 million three-phase Lobito Corridor reconstruction program consisting of renovation of the Benguela railway, modernization of the port of Lobito, and the rehabilitation of the Lomaum power station along with investment in telecommunications and roadworks.

Despite the foregoing, however, such short-term factors as the renewed war, depressed world prices for copper, and the unstable political situation in Zaire make it highly questionable whether much would be gained by attempting to rebuild the Benguela railroad before the end of the century. A recent World Bank survey called for a less energetic approach to linking the coast to Huambo and Cuito in the center of the country. Noting infrastructural decay, the Bank has been examining an 18-month, $30 million rehabilitation program for this area.

Ports

Angola has three main ports (Luanda, Lobito, and Namibe) as well as smaller ones in Cabinda, Soyo, and Porto Amboim. During the colonial era, the Portuguese developed each of the ports in tandem with a rail line to facilitate increased exports of the country's diverse resources. Because the civil war severely limited seaborne exports, the ports have been primarily used to import supplies and food in the postcolonial period. In 1973, Angola's ports processed 6.4 million tons of goods, of which 90 percent were exports. In 1986, the same ports handled only 1.6 million tons of goods, of which nearly 90 percent were imports (these figures do not include military hardware). All of the ports are in need of maintenance, technical assistance, and replacement parts.

Luanda was developed into a deep-water port in 1945 to accommodate large ships and to handle the annual exportation of 80 percent of the coffee crop. Commercial traffic peaked in 1973 at 2,324,000 tons; by 1985, it had fallen to 942,000 tons. Imports (mostly food and consumer products) exceed exports by an eight-to-one ratio. Like all of Angola's ports, Luanda is handicapped by inadequate unloading, storage, and transportation facilities and by an undertrained and poorly paid work force. These shortcomings result in theft and long delays in unloading goods, primarily from container traffic; at one point in 1981,

90 ships were waiting in the harbor to be unloaded. The decline in imports, as a result of the decline in oil revenues, has reduced some of the congestion. Still, the collateral impact of the problems at Luanda harbor echoes strongly throughout the economy: most manufacturing operations are based in Luanda, and the government imports most of the country's needs through the capital port. The World Bank has already designated nearly $5 million to develop a comprehensive strategy for the rehabilitation and expansion of Luanda harbor.

In 1973, the port of Lobito handled 2,545,000 tons of commercial freight. Traffic dropped to 522,000 tons by 1985 and 440,000 tons by 1987, of which 90 percent was imports. Lobito is the only Angolan port to possess facilities appropriate for storage of imports, and even these are in need of increased capacity. Lobito also has a large (unused) ore-loading facility, quayside rail service, eight berths for freighters, and a tanker terminal for the off-loading of petroleum products. The World Bank is expected to provide up to $8 million for the rehabilitation of the Lobito port along with the European Union, which recently pledged $20 million. The SADC rehabilitation program for the Lobito corridor also envisages upgrading both its export and import capabilities.

In the 1950s, the Portuguese utilized what is now the port of Namibe (formerly Moçâmedes) to export iron ore transported by rail from the mines at Cassinga. In 1973, over 97.5 percent of the 6,379,000 tons exported through the port consisted of iron ore. In 1985, the port handled only 171,000 tons of goods, of which 6,000 tons were exports. By 1990, that figure had fallen to less than 150,000 tons. The World Bank has already provided $2.3 million for refurbishing the port and improving its human resource capacity.

Two studies on the rehabilitation of Angola's ports have been undertaken by foreign companies—VEB-Industrie Konsult Berlin of former East Germany and Ramboll & Hannemon of Denmark. Many of their recommendations (such as the construction of modern container terminals in each port) are, however, precluded by serious budgetary restraints. Thus far, there appears to have been limited outside interest in taking on the task of rebuilding Angola's port system.

Airlines

The Portuguese began air service between Luanda, Huambo, and Moçâmedes (Namibe) in 1940. In 1977, the MPLA government formed a national airline, Linhas Aéreas de Angola (TAAG). Flying has been the only transportation subsector to show steady growth since independence.

TAAG's freight traffic increased almost 20 percent (to 35,000 tons) from 1980 to 1986, while passenger travel over the same period increased at an annual rate of 15 percent, reaching more than 1 million by the end of the period. In terms of value, TAAG ships 45 percent of all goods transported by any method. The Luanda-Lisbon route is the busiest TAAG service, accounting for 36 percent of all passenger travel and 42 percent of all cargo transported. Prior to the devaluation of the kwanza, a Luanda-Lisbon passenger ticket could be purchased for the equivalent of one case (24 cans) of beer on the parallel market.

TAAG's fleet as of 1991 consisted of six Boeing 707s constructed in the 1960s, five Boeing 737s built during the late 1970s and early 1980s, five Fokker F27s built from 1969 to 1982, two Yak-40s of 1977 vintage, and an inoperable Lockheed L100. TAAG also owns 10 light aircraft used on shorter domestic flights. The Boeing 737 is TAAG's workhorse, accounting for the largest number of landings as well as crashes (three Boeing 737s have been lost). The on-time performance of the airline is rated at 32 percent for international flights (Africa, Europe, and South America) and 56 percent for domestic.

TAAG has recently shown interest in purchasing new aircraft from either Airbus Industries or Boeing for its aging fleet, much of which may be banned from overflying Europe due to noise restrictions. Decreased oil revenues, however, appear to preclude the purchase of any additional aircraft at this time. TAAG currently wet-leases (i.e., leases with a full service contract) planes for overseas travel through the Portuguese state airline TAP.

A shortage of managerial and technical skills among TAAG's 5,400 employees compounds the airline's operational problems. Another complication is that the hub airport in Luanda must be relied upon for most services that would normally be available at regional airports (e.g., refueling, maintenance, and storage).

Despite all its weaknesses, TAAG has played (and continues to play) a critical role in the Angolan economy. Prior to the resumption of fighting in 1992, TAAG regularly serviced all key provincial cities. During the pre-1992 phase of the civil war, the airline provided the only dependable form of transportation for people and supplies when ground travel was restricted. Since the resumption of war, TAAG's domestic flights have been limited to coastal cities.

13

Conclusion

As of spring 1994, there is increasing optimism that peace talks between the Angolan government and UNITA in Lusaka, Zambia will yield a comprehensive settlement bringing lasting peace to this war-torn country. Agreement has been reached on a wide range of substantive issues, including military and police matters. The remaining issues to be resolved include national reconciliation and the completion of the electoral process begun in September 1992. The two sides have progressed well beyond the conceptual phase on these points and are negotiating detailed positions and timetables for implementation.

The role of the United Nations will be an important element of the overall Lusaka Accord. Immediately upon the signature of an agreement in Lusaka, the UN Security Council will meet to authorize the deployment of a UN military force for Angola under the auspices of UNAVEM III. The deployment of a comprehensive UNAVEM III force will occur as follows:

1. within 10 days, 100 military troops will be sent to Angola,
2. within 30 days, 350 additional troops and 126 police observers along with 14 medical personnel will be deployed, and
3. 60 to 90 days from the meeting of the Security Council, an estimated 6,000 troops are scheduled to be dispatched to Angola as part of the overall Lusaka Accord.

Also, 10 days following the initialing of the Lusaka Accord, representatives of the Angolan government and UNITA will meet in São Tomé & Príncipe under UN auspices to finalize the details of the military and police framework agreed on in Lusaka. Five days have been allotted for this complicated and detailed process although it is expected to require additional time. An official signing ceremony, possibly carried out by President dos Santos and Savimbi, should occur within 30 days of the initialing of the accord.

It is only through the creation of a global peace accord in Angola that the difficult task of rebuilding the economy of this potentially wealthy nation can begin. In addition to that long-awaited and critical step, however, careful economic planning, commitment to reform, and strong diversification of foreign investment in all sectors are also necessary if sustainable development is to occur in this resource-rich southern African nation. There is optimism that the Economic and Social Program of 1994 recently launched by the Angolan government will serve as a framework for the reconstruction of the country, but these hopes must be tempered with the reality that substantive reform will occur only with the support of the political leadership.

Through a comprehensive sectoral analysis of its economy and its prospects for growth in a postwar environment, it is possible to envisage that Angola—former Portuguese colony for nearly 500 years, playground of the cold war for more than three decades, and forgotten battlefield that has claimed 500,000 lives—easily possesses the potential to become one of Africa's wealthiest nations and an engine for dynamic regional economic growth.

Sources

The research materials used in the preparation of this volume include the following:

Angola: An Introductory Economic Review, Volumes I and II (United Nations Development Program/World Bank, Report No. 7283–ANG, June 26, 1989).
Angola: An Introductory Economic Review, Volumes I and II (World Bank, Report No. 8906–ANG, June 29, 1990).
Angola: Issues and Options in the Energy Sector (Joint United Nations Development Program/World Bank Energy Sector Assessment Program, Report No. 7408–ANG, May 1989).
Tony Hodges, *Angola to 2000: Prospects for Recovery* (Research Report, The Economist Intelligence Unit, February 1993).
The Economist Intelligence Unit's quarterly and annual country reports on Angola from 1985 through 1994.
J. C. Victor de Carvalho, *Economic Memorandum on the People's Republic of Angola* (Embassy of the People's Republic of Angola, London, July 1992).
Various other books, chapters, and papers, of which some of the most helpful were Gerald J. Bender, *Angola Under the Portuguese: The Myth and the Reality* (University of California Press, 1978); Keith Sommerville, *Angola: Politics, Economics, and Society* (Lynne Rienner Publishers, 1986); J. G. Rebelo, "Contribution to the History of Petroleum Industry in Angola 1910–1987" (paper presented at the meeting of the SPE, Angola Section, April 29, 1988); Graham Walker, *Angola: The Promise of Riches* (Africa File Ltd., 1990); Gillian Gunn, "The Angolan Economy: A Status Report," *CSIS Africa Notes* no. 58, May 1986; Shawn McCormick, "Angola in Transition: The Cabinda Factor," *CSIS Africa Notes* no. 137, June 1992; and "The Angolan Economy: A History of Contradictions," in *Afro-Marxist Regimes,* Edmond J. Keller

and Donald Rothchild, eds. (Lynne Rienner Publishers, 1987).

A wide range of newspaper and periodical articles, notably from *African Research Bulletin: Economic Series* (Basil Blackwell, Oxford, U.K.), *The Southern African Economist* (Harare, Zimbabwe), and *Foreign Broadcast Information Service Daily Report: Sub-Saharan Africa* (Springfield, Virginia).

Personal interviews with officials of corporations (including Chevron, Texaco, Conoco, Leon Tempelsman & Son, and Société Générale de Belgique), academicians (notably Gerald J. Bender and John A. Marcum), representatives of international organizations involved in Angola (including the World Bank, the International Monetary Fund, the European Union, the International Committee of the Red Cross, and Catholic Relief Services), and officials of the United States, Angola (both MPLA and UNITA), Portugal, Great Britain, France, Belgium, Brazil, and South Africa.

When information obtained from different sources was contradictory, UN Development Program/World Bank data were used.

Appendix
Key Dates in the History of Angola

1951. Portugal's five colonies in Africa (Angola, Mozambique, Guinea-Bissau, São Tomé & Príncipe, and Cape Verde) are officially incorporated into the Portuguese state.

December 1956. The Movimento Popular de Libertação de Angola (MPLA) is founded.

1961. On February 4, an organized attack on the main political prison in Luanda marks the beginning of open resistance to colonial rule. The outbreak of widespread insurrection in the north on March 15 elicits a massive response from the Portuguese. As many as 20,000 Africans are killed in the following six months.

March 1962. Two northern-based parties merge to form the Frente Nacional de Libertação de Angola (FNLA) under the leadership of Holden Roberto.

March 1966. Jonas Savimbi forms the Unio Nacional para a Independência Total de Angola (UNITA).

April 25, 1974. After 13 years of dealing with armed insurrection in Portuguese-ruled Africa, an Armed Forces Movement led by war-weary officers overthrows the authoritarian Caetano regime in Lisbon and subsequently undertakes to wind down the Portuguese presence on the continent. At this point, neither the United States nor the Soviet Union is actively involved in supporting their traditional allies, the FNLA and MPLA respectively.

1975. On January 15, the new Portuguese government signs an agreement with leaders of the MPLA, UNITA, and the FNLA at Alvor (Portugal) providing for a transitional coalition government comprising the three groups and setting November

---

Entries for 1951 through May 25, 1991 based on centerfold feature in "Angola: The Road to Peace," *CSIS Africa Notes* no. 125, June 1991.

11 as the date of Angolan independence. In late January, the U.S. National Security Council's "40 Committee" authorizes covert assistance in the amount of $300,000 to the FNLA. In the following months, Soviet arms deliveries to the MPLA increase. The agreement reached at Alvor breaks down as conflict among the MPLA, UNITA, and FNLA forces escalates. Assistance from external sources (the United States, Zaire, and South Africa for the FNLA and later UNITA; the Soviet Union and Cuba for the MPLA) becomes an increasingly important factor. On October 14, a South African-led motorized force enters Angola from Namibia in support of the FNLA and UNITA. On November 11, following the departure of the Portuguese high commissioner and his staff from Luanda, the MPLA, backed by Cuban troops, proclaims the establishment of the People's Republic of Angola with Agostinho Neto as president.

Early 1976. Between January and March, South Africa (whose troops had stalled in mid-November some 120 miles south of Luanda in the face of an entrenched MPLA force with Cuban reinforcements) withdraws to Namibia. In February, the MPLA achieves an apparent military victory, having ended the FNLA's role as a serious contender and driven the remnants of UNITA's army into the southeastern bush.

February 11, 1976. The MPLA regime is accorded membership in the Organization of African Unity.

June 30, 1976. President Gerald Ford reluctantly signs into law legislation passed by Congress (the Clark Amendment) that prohibits any security assistance to groups in Angola "unless and until the Congress expressly authorizes such assistance by law."

October 1976. The MPLA government signs a treaty of friendship and cooperation with the Soviet Union.

May 27, 1977. A coup attempt by Nito Alves, the reputedly pro-Soviet leader of a dissident MPLA faction, is thwarted. Soviet and Cuban complicity in the takeover bid is charged and both ambassadors are expelled; Cuban troops ultimately help to defeat the rebellion.

December 1977. At its first national party congress, the MPLA proclaims itself a Marxist-Leninist party oriented toward "scientific socialism."

1978. South Africa begins a series of military incursions into Angolan territory, allegedly to target South West Africa People's Organization (SWAPO) guerrillas seeking to end Pretoria's control over Namibia.

September 10, 1979. President Neto dies of pancreatic cancer in a Moscow hospital and is succeeded by Minister of Planning José Eduardo dos Santos.

March 19, 1981. The Reagan administration formally submits to Congress a proposal that the Clark Amendment be repealed, but the request is soundly defeated.

August 1981. Operation Protea, which commits as many as 11,000 South African troops some 75 miles into Angola, signals an escalation of South African cross-border action—action now aimed as much against MPLA as against SWAPO targets. Meanwhile, UNITA (with considerable assistance from South Africa) is reviving as a military threat to the regime.

January 1982. South African and Cuban troops clash on the Angolan-Namibian border for the first time in over six years.

February 16, 1984. Representatives of the Angolan and South African governments, meeting under the chairmanship of Zambia's President Kenneth Kaunda, sign the U.S.-brokered Lusaka Accord. South Africa agrees to withdraw its military presence from southern Angola; the MPLA undertakes to restrict SWAPO activities in the area bordering Namibia.

May 21, 1985. An Angolan military patrol captures a South African commando unit near oil storage tanks in the Cabinda enclave. Its leader, Captain Wynand du Toit, subsequently admits that the unit had planned to blow up the tanks and leave UNITA propaganda at the scene to make it appear that UNITA was responsible. He also indicates that South Africa is responsible for some past sabotage that UNITA has claimed.

June 1985. South Africa resumes "hot-pursuit" operations into Angola.

July 10, 1985. The U.S. House of Representatives votes 236 to 185 to repeal the Clark Amendment; this step follows a 63 to 34 repeal vote in the Senate on June 11. The Reagan administration is now free to renew U.S. assistance to UNITA.

January 30, 1986. President Ronald Reagan meets with Savimbi at the White House and reaffirms support for UNITA.

February 18, 1986. Testifying before the Senate Foreign Relations Committee, Assistant Secretary of State for African Affairs Chester Crocker acknowledges that the Reagan administration has decided to give covert military aid (including antitank weapons and antiaircraft missiles) to UNITA. "The process is in motion," he says.

1987. The MPLA launches the largest offensive to date against the UNITA stronghold at Mavinga, but is repulsed by South African and UNITA forces.

December 22, 1988. More than seven years of wide-ranging negotiations orchestrated by Crocker culminate in the signature in New York of a tripartite agreement by Angola, Cuba, and South Africa, as well as a bilateral agreement between Angola and Cuba. These agreements provide, inter alia, for the withdrawal of Cuban troops from Angola over a 27-month period and the withdrawal of South African troops from neighboring Namibia. On the basis of the New York accords, Namibia's transition to independence in accordance with UN Security Council Resolution 435 is completed on March 21, 1990.

January 6, 1989. In a private letter to Savimbi, President-elect George Bush says that the United States will continue its support for UNITA until national reconciliation is achieved in Angola.

January 27, 1989. In a sharp break with past policy, the MPLA indicates that it is prepared to seek a political solution to the war.

March 13, 1989. Savimbi calls for direct dialogue with the MPLA and offers to exclude himself from the negotiations and from a subsequent transitional government as it prepares for elections. He also proposes a four-month cease-fire.

May 4, 1989. Ambassador Herman J. Cohen, testifying before the Senate Foreign Relations Committee on his nomination to succeed Crocker as assistant secretary of state for African affairs, says that there will be no change in the U.S. policy of providing support to UNITA or denying diplomatic recognition to the MPLA government until Angola's warring parties reach a political settlement.

June 22, 1989. Dos Santos and Savimbi agree to a cease-fire at a meeting hosted by Zaire's President Mobutu Sese Seko in Gbadolite. The agreement is subsequently derailed, however, when UNITA learns that Mobutu erroneously informed the MPLA that Savimbi had also agreed to several additional conditions, including the incorporation of UNITA into the MPLA and his exile for an unspecified period. Matters are further confused when it surfaces that Mobutu told UNITA that the MPLA had agreed to the guerrillas' platform for negotiations, including cease-fire terms, formation of a government of national unity, and the holding of elections.

July 18, 1989. The International Monetary Fund admits Angola as its 152nd member by a vote of 136 to 1. The United States casts the only negative vote.

December 23, 1989. With Soviet military assistance, the MPLA launches a large-scale assault against the UNITA-controlled town of Mavinga in southeastern Angola. Although Savimbi's forces are almost dislodged at the outset, the battle grinds to a stalemate with heavy casualties on both sides.

Early April 1990. Both the MPLA and UNITA publicly state their desire for a negotiated solution to the war.

April 24–25, 1990. Portugal's Secretary of State for Foreign Affairs and Cooperation José Durão Barroso convenes near Lisbon the first in a series of face-to-face negotiating sessions between representatives of the MPLA and UNITA.

October 17, 1990. By a vote of 207 to 206, the U.S. House of Representatives passes an amendment proposed by Rep. Stephen Solarz (D-New York) to the annual Intelligence Authorization bill. The amendment called for the suspension of covert lethal aid to UNITA if the MPLA agreed to a cease-fire and proposed a "reasonable timetable" for elections. President Bush subsequently vetoes the legislation.

November 1990. U.S. Secretary of State James A. Baker III and then-Soviet Foreign Minister Eduard Shevardnadze agree to become actively involved in furthering Portuguese mediation efforts after a fifth round of peace talks fails to yield concrete results.

December 6, 1990. UNITA says it will agree to a cease-fire if the MPLA approves a multiparty system at its third Party Congress.

December 10, 1990. The MPLA Party Congress votes to revise the Angolan constitution to allow for a two-phase (rather than an immediate) transition to a multiparty system. This action falls short of UNITA's demand for endorsement of a multiparty system.

December 12, 1990. Baker meets with Angolan Minister of External Relations Pedro de Castro dos Santos Van-Dúnem ("Loy") at the State Department while Shevardnadze meets with Savimbi at the Soviet Embassy in Washington. The following day, the participants in these conversations, joined by Portuguese officials, meet at the State Department and draw up a set of peace "concepts" around which the timing of a cease-fire and a date for elections can be worked out.

January 10, 1991. Portuguese, U.S., and Soviet representatives meet in Lisbon to refine the peace "concepts" agreement before a scheduled sixth round of MPLA-UNITA talks in the Portuguese capital.

February 8, 1991. Following three days of intensive consultations by Portuguese diplomats with both sides, the decision is made not to convene the planned sixth round of peace talks because of an unexpected announcement by the MPLA that it is unwilling to sign the "concepts" agreement until UNITA agrees to a date for a cease-fire.

April 4, 1991. The sixth round of Portuguese-mediated talks between the MPLA and UNITA finally gets under way, ushering in an open-ended series of meetings aimed at finding a negotiated solution to the war.

April 28, 1991. At the end of a special five-day Party Congress, the MPLA approves a change in the Angolan constitution that replaces the designation "Marxism-Leninism" with "democratic socialism."

May 1, 1991. MPLA and UNITA representatives meeting in Portugal initial a peace agreement.

May 15, 1991. Although sporadic fighting continues, a de facto cease-fire between UNITA and the MPLA begins.

May 25, 1991. Cuba withdraws the last of its 50,000 troops from Angola, more than a month ahead of the departure date specified in the December 1988 Angola-Namibia accords.

May 31, 1991. The Bicesse Peace Accords initialed on May 1 are formally signed in Lisbon by Angola's President José Eduardo dos Santos and UNITA leader Jonas Savimbi. The agreement specifies a timetable for the laying down of arms; unifying the two armies into one Angolan Armed Forces (FAA); and the holding of national elections to be monitored by the United Nations.

June 17, 1991. The Joint Political Commission (JPCM or CCPM), comprised of members from MPLA and UNITA and observers from the United States, the Soviet Union, and Portugal is inaugurated to supervise the Peace Accords process.

August 1, 1991. The first important deadline in the military dimension of the peace process is not realized and the self-implementing nature of the Bicesse Accords shows stress when both the government and UNITA fail to place all of their troops in the 48 established containment areas.

September 26, 1991. Dos Santos visits Washington for the first time and meets with President George Bush. The Angolan president announces that elections will take place in September 1992.

September 29, 1991. Savimbi returns to Luanda for the first time since 1975.

Late October, 1991. The Angolan government and UNITA agree on various elements concerning the composition of the

FAA. The structure includes 40,000 army, 6,000 air force, and 4,000 navy posts.

December 5, 1991. The Angolan government submits a formal request to the UN for technical assistance in the electoral process.

January 14, 1992. First all-party forum held in Luanda to discuss the electoral process, electoral law, and the role of the National Electoral Council (CNE).

March 6, 1992. UN Secretary General Boutros Boutros-Ghali outlines a plan for the UN to monitor the Angolan elections. At this time the UN Angola Verification Mission (UNAVEM) consists of 350 military observers and support personnel, but expands the electoral division into regional staff offices covering all 18 of the country's provinces. Margaret Anstee, special representative of the UN secretary general, arrives in Luanda.

March 25, 1992. After fleeing Angola in late February and early March, UNITA Foreign Minister Tony da Costa Fernandes and Interior Minister General Miguel N'Zau Puna accuse Savimbi of personal involvement in human rights violations against senior UNITA members and their families, including former Washington representative Tito Chingunji and Lisbon representative Wilson dos Santos.

March 31, 1992. The formal process of demobilizing government and UNITA troops begins after extensive delays.

April 1992. The People's Assembly enacts an Electoral Law to serve as the legal framework for an election organization and to set its guidelines and modalities.

May 9, 1992. The independent CNE is sworn in with Onofre dos Santos, a former FNLA official, appointed as director general.

May 20, 1992. The voter registration period begins and is scheduled to last until July 31.

July 31, 1992. The voter registration period is extended for two weeks. More than 90 percent (5.1 million) of eligible Angolans register to vote. None of the political parties lodges a formal complaint regarding the process.

August 29, 1992. The official election campaign period for political parties begins.

September 29–30, 1992. In a climate of peace, tolerance, and optimism, nationwide presidential and legislative elections are held under the observation of 800 international observers. More than 4,000 of the 5,800 polling sites are visited by the impartial observers. Nearly 95 percent of registered voters cast ballots.

October 3, 1992. As ballots continue to be counted and results released on a trailing basis, Savimbi breaks the national sense of optimism by attacking, in a sharply worded national radio address, the impartiality of the electoral process with claims of widespread and systematic voter irregularities. The United Nations, in coordination with the CNE, begins an investigation that finds no conclusive evidence to support Savimbi's claims.

October 5, 1992. UNITA's top generals withdraw from the FAA, citing electoral fraud. Tensions heighten throughout the country.

October 7, 1992. The government invites UNITA to join a government of national unity if it accepts electoral defeat. In a move welcomed by international observers, UNITA agrees to take part in four commissions of inquiry investigating Savimbi's allegations of fraud. UNITA also agrees to accept arbitration by UNAVEM II, which oversees the committees.

October 11–14, 1992. In an effort to avert a resumption of war, the UN Security Council dispatches to Angola an ad hoc commission of representatives from the United States, Russia, Morocco, and Cape Verde. UNITA troops are reportedly leaving various containment areas across the nation.

October 16, 1992. Boutros-Ghali telephones Savimbi to inform him personally that, although the MPLA won a majority in the legislative elections, President dos Santos did not receive the mandated 50 percent vote total necessary to avoid a run-off in the presidential election. According to Angolan electoral law, a second round of presidential elections is necessary within 30 days.

October 17, 1992. Election results are officially announced. President dos Santos receives 49.57 percent of the presidential vote, and Savimbi receives 40.07 percent. In the legislative vote, the MPLA receives 53.47 percent to UNITA's 34.10 percent. Anstee declares the elections "generally free and fair." Meanwhile, UNITA launches military operations to occupy municipalities and remove local administrators across the country. Fearful that UNITA may attempt to take Luanda, the government begins dispensing weapons to its supporters in the capital.

October 20, 1992. The troika of representatives (United States, Portugal, Russia) meets with both Savimbi and dos Santos in separate sessions urging the two to meet face-to-face.

Savimbi maintains that the elections were a massive fraud, but announces his willingness to accept a runoff in the presidential election.

October 21, 1992. Government and UNITA representatives convene in Luanda for extended discussions regarding the holding of a run-off presidential election.

October 31, 1992. Remnants of the national army and newly armed MPLA supporters in various cities (including Luanda) attack UNITA. Several thousand people are killed, including a significant number of senior UNITA officials in Luanda. Among those dead are UNITA Vice President Jeremias Chitunda and UNITA Representative to the Joint-Political Military Commission Salupeto Pena.

November 2, 1992. The joint efforts of Boutros-Ghali, Anstee, and diplomats from various nations achieve agreement on an official cease-fire.

November 5, 1992. UN Under Secretary General for Peacekeeping Marrack Goulding arrives in Angola to assist Anstee in negotiating with both sides in an effort to put peace back on track.

November 26, 1992. Anstee meets with government and UNITA representatives in the southern port city of Namibe, where a tentative agreement is reached to end the fighting. Within hours, UNITA forces invalidate the Namibe agreement when they occupy the northern cities of Uige and Negage. Fighting between the two sides resumes.

Early December 1992. Militarily, UNITA is in control of more territory at this point than at any time in the course of its 26-year existence. The government possesses control of Luanda and its environs, areas immediately along the coast, and various provincial capitals in the central and southern portions of the country. Disorganized government troops prepare for a counter attack against UNITA as the dos Santos regime begins purchasing weapons from abroad.

January 9, 1993. Government forces inside the central city of Huambo attack UNITA positions around the city limits. Within days, heavy fighting breaks out in 10 provincial capitals and several other population centers.

January 21, 1993. Boutros-Ghali states in a report to the United Nations that "Angola has returned to civil war." The UNAVEM II mission is significantly reduced.

January 27–30, 1993. Anstee convenes direct talks between government and UNITA representatives in Addis Ababa, Ethiopia. The two parties disagree on terms of a cease-fire but agree to meet again the following month. Fighting continues unabated across the country.

February 26, 1993. Anstee is forced to cancel the second round of Addis Ababa talks when UNITA fails to send its delegation.

March 6, 1993. Huambo, Angola's second largest city and heart of the Ovimbundu people, falls to UNITA forces. Government forces and thousands of civilians flee to the coastal city of Benguela.

April 12, 1993. New UN-sponsored talks directed by Anstee begin in Abidjan, Côte d'Ivoire.

May 19, 1993. The United States accords official recognition to the government of Angola for the first time since its inception in November 1975.

May 21, 1993. As an accord on 38 general principles is about to be reached following six weeks of often difficult negotiations in Abidjan, Anstee reluctantly suspends the talks when it becomes clear that UNITA refuses to accept two final points, which would have had UNITA move its troops from urban areas to cantonment sites and demobilize military personnel not selected for the FAA. Fighting quickly escalates across the country, with an estimated 1,000 people dying each day either directly or indirectly due to the war.

June 7, 1993. FAA Chief of Staff General João de Matos announces in Lisbon that the government has formally revoked the triple zero arms embargo of the Bicesse Accords. Both the government and UNITA have reportedly violated the agreement for several months.

June 28, 1993. Boutros-Ghali appoints Maître Alioune Blondin Beye of Mali to succeed Anstee, whose tenure as special representative of the secretary general had expired.

August 4, 1993. Savimbi's birthday festivities in Huambo are disrupted by government bombing raids. Fighting in Cuito intensifies as famine conditions are reported in that city.

August 11, 1993. Savimbi calls for unconditional peace talks with the government as it continues shelling Cuito with an estimated 1,500 rounds per day.

September 15, 1993. Under U.S. leadership, the UN Security Council adopts Resolution 864 prohibiting the sale and supply of any military and petroleum products to UNITA. The first-ever UN sanctions against UNITA are to take effect in 10 days.

September 20, 1993. UNITA declares a unilateral ceasefire. Fighting does not end but subsides for the next few months.

September 25, 1993. As the UN sanctions take effect, Beye and foreign diplomats hold talks with UNITA in São Tomé. The talks are boycotted by the Angolan government.

October 6, 1993. UNITA's Central Committee issues a communiqué restating the set of principles agreed to in Abidjan but includes acceptance of withdrawing its forces from urban areas to cantonment sites.

October 25, 1993. In Lusaka, Zambia, Beye convenes closed-door exploratory talks between delegations of both parties.

November 15, 1993. Closed-door peace talks between the Angolan government and UNITA officials begin under UN auspices.

December 13, 1993. Following clear progress on military matters in the peace talks, the government presents its first proposal for a national reconciliation government to Beye.

January 31, 1994. Government and UNITA negotiators agree on the composition of both the police and anti-riot forces. The path is open to discuss national reconciliation.

March 6, 1994. The government restates its December 13 proposal on national reconciliation to the mediators with only slight revisions. UNITA formally counterproposes various government posts on March 10 and again on March 17.

April 6, 1994. A deadlock in the Lusaka peace talks over the issue of national reconciliation prompts a recess. Beye travels to Geneva to consult with Boutros-Ghali.

May 25, 1994. Four weeks after President Bill Clinton writes to him, President dos Santos responds favorably to the appeal to accept a final compromise proposal on national reconciliation arranged by the mediators in Lusaka. Full details are not disclosed.

May 31, 1994. The UN Security Council is scheduled to discuss the peace process in Lusaka and consider the extension of the UNAVEM II mandate.